Treasured Silence

During a short recess, our fractured lives
found safety and comfort

Angela Carbajal Detloff

Treasured Silence

During a short recess, our fractured lives found safety and comfort

ISBN 978 0 692 99345 3

© 2018 by Angela Carbajal Detloff

All rights reserved. This book or any portion thereof may not be reproduced or used in any manner whatsoever without the express written permission of the author except for the use of brief citations in a book review or scholarly journal.

Art cover design by Michael Spader

Spaderart@gmail.com

Published by Angela Carbajal Detloff in Hillsboro, New Mexico. 2018

CONTENTS

Prologue	i
Forward	ii
Acknowledgements	iii
Author's Note	iv
Chapter One. Who Am I?	1
Chapter Two. 1938 Mom & Dad	4
Chapter Three. My Early Years	9
Chapter Four. Floods in Town	14
Chapter Five. Johnny's Café	16
Chapter Six. Mother Married Joe	18
Chapter Seven. Mother Pregnant	20
Chapter Eight. 1956 Stinking Drunk	22
Chapter Nine. Toys, what Toys?	25
Chapter Ten. Beth's Wedding	26
Chapter Eleven. Unworthy	27
Chapter Twelve. Middle School	30
Chapter Thirteen. Angel in the Car	34
Chapter Fourteen. My Eighteen Year Plan	37
Chapter Fifteen. My Wedding	40
Chapter Sixteen. My Son Armando	45
Chapter Seventeen. Therapy 1971	51
Chapter Eighteen. Christiaan	55

Chapter Nineteen. Our Princess_____59

Chapter Twenty. Therapy 1982_____62

Chapter Twenty-one. Major Roadblock_____72

Chapter Twenty-two. 1989 Thrown to the Wolf_____75

Chapter Twenty-three. Throw the Pan_____80

Chapter Twenty-four. Successes_____83

Chapter Twenty-five. He's an Oak_____86

Chapter Twenty-six. Stirring_____88

Chapter Twenty-seven. Cancer & Redemption _____94

Chapter Twenty-eight. Unexplainable Yearning_____96

Chapter Twenty-nine. Mother was Always Angry_____101

Chapter Thirty. An Advocate_____103

Chapter Thirty-one. Closure_____105

Chapter Thirty-two. Role Model_____107

Chapter Thirty-three. Dad's Family_____109

Chapter Thirty-four. Missed Opportunities_____111

Chapter Thirty-five. My Fantasy World_____113

Chapter Thirty-six. The Barbershop Cafe_____115

Chapter Thirty-seven. Prophetic Visions_____117

Chapter Thirty-eight. Redeem, forgive & repent_____120

Chapter Thirty-nine. Bonnie_____121

Chapter Forty. My Best Friend_____124

Epilogue_____128

PROLOGUE

"No!" I wailed, "Please don't leave me, Daddy" I held tightly to his leg, crying loudly. My sobs only caused my mother's heart to harden more.

She was telling him to go. "Leave now and don't come back here, ever! I am getting a divorce. You need to go!" she shouted at him, pulling me away.

I crumpled to the floor. Even at the age of three, I understood how final this encounter was. Somehow, my mind was able to grasp just what this would mean for me and our family. Through blurry eyes, I tried to memorize all the details I could take in, and even now I see his beautifully polished brown wingtips with tiny holes cut into the leather for the laces and the added detail on the tips.

To assure he would never find us, Mother moved us around a lot, mostly within New Mexico but all the way to Los Angeles as well. At times we lived in rundown houses, or crowded into ugly sheds in questionable neighborhoods. But there were far worse events on the horizon than these.

I remember clearly the day my daddy left; the memory is imbedded in my mind as though it was yesterday.

I have very few memories of the proceeding years and then almost as if suddenly I'm nine years old. The nosebleeds and hospital visits are clear in my mind. The times alone with my mother are a complete blank.

FOREWORD

New Mexico is known for the Spanish Entrada, with its depredations on the Pueblo Indians. Their descendants and descendants of my Native American ancestors still reside in the state. New Mexico is also famous for many Wild West stories and Billy the Kid. The first Atomic Bomb was tested northwest of Alamogordo at the Trinity Site. Along with stories of witchcraft and the supernatural, New Mexico has hosted artists such as Georgia O'Keeffe, Elliot Porter, Luis Jimenez and many others.

The most profound thing about this "Land of Enchantment" is the untouched, unfettered brilliant blue sky by day. At night the stars paint a glorious bounty of twinkle lights on a striking black canvas. I have such gratitude for the magnificent splendor of the world that we live in.

My story begins in the small town of Hillsboro, that had its own legends. There was the hanging tree, a landmark for decades, and at least one house that boasted of a trap door used for escape when the Indians attacked.

ACKNOWLEDGEMENTS

I would like to acknowledge the following individuals that have read my story and supported me in this endeavor.

First and foremost I thank my husband Steve for being the driving force behind self-doubt that I could accomplish this project. It has been on the back burner since about 1983.

Secondly, my appreciation and thanks go to Harley Shaw and Patty Woodruff. They are two of the most sought out individuals, with raw editing skills; when someone wishes true honest feedback. I was concerned that when I gave them my first manuscript they would look at it and tell me to go do something else; they didn't, instead they supported and encouraged me; both felt that my story needed to be told.

I would also like to acknowledge my Sozo facilitator, Thomas Brustad for his encouragement and support.

AUTHOR'S NOTE

Everything in this book is true, some names have been changed out of respect for privacy.

CHAPTER ONE
Who Am I?

My name is Angela. The question of who I am is critical because as I traveled on my journey to healing and wholeness there were times that I didn't know who I was or would I remain broken. I am the fourth daughter born to my family. My parents were so certain of having a boy that they could call "Angel"; my given name came as close as possible to their disappointed dream. My sisters are Beth, Bonnie and Bibiana. We are each two-to-three years apart.

My oldest sister was born at home in the little adobe house that grandfather built. She was so tiny at three pounds that her bed was made from an old shoebox. Her tiny baby bonnet would fit a tennis ball.

In spirit I knew that mother desperately wanted a son. My parents may have thought that a son was the savior that would change their lives and maybe, repair their broken marriage. A son might change things where as another girl was an encumbrance.

When mother was pregnant with me close to her due date she was overwhelmingly tired. Her doctor discovered that she was anemic and both she and I had a faint heart. Mother received blood transfusions and injections round the clock to prevent a miscarriage. She weighed only ninety-five pounds. Because she was so malnourished, I was born frail with many infirmities. I was a sickly child and consequently spent much time seeing doctors and getting medical care. The nosebleeds hemorrhaged regularly and I had frequent bouts of pneumonia. However, I learned that the hospital turned out to be a safe and fun place.

My story begins in a small mining town in Southwest New Mexico. In 1877 gold and silver were discovered and overnight it became a boomtown. The area would remain prosperous until the decline of the mines. When the jobs could not sustain the families, many moved out of state, primarily to California, with dreams of finding sustainable work.

My oldest sister Beth is kind to a fault. She is fair skinned and in her youth reminded you of the screen actresses of the 1940's. The next in line is Bonnie, very insecure and occasionally thinks of herself as a victim. When she was young she had a striking resemblance in looks and figure to the Italian actress Sophia Loren. She had those same stunning eyes. Then there's Bibiana, she was always mom's favorite. Maybe it is her beautiful blue eyes. Mother couldn't do enough for her always boasting about how smart she is. She is smart but when it came to Bibiana mother only saw her while wearing rose colored glasses. In their youth any of my sisters could have made the cover of Vogue Magazine as they are all strikingly beautiful each in her own way. After mother passed away Beth stepped in to fill the gap upholding Bibiana as the favored one and seeing her only through the same rose colored glasses.

We attended school in New Mexico and sometimes in California. After I turned thirteen I never wanted to visit New Mexico as there were far too many painful memories attached to our home town; it would be decades before I would ever return.

While growing up I often heard stories about the witchcraft that existed in New Mexico. In the United States people often think of the Salem Witch Trials of the earlier centuries. However, many of the people living in New Mexico believed in and practiced witchcraft. Then there is the spirit of poverty that is still prevalent. Rarely did anyone talk about God; I desired and needed so much more.

CHAPTER TWO
1938 Mom & Dad

Both of my parents were born in the Southwest. My fathers name is Juan and, he was born in Kelly, New Mexico on October 8, 1917. My mother Sophie was born in Chloride, New Mexico on March 15, 1919.

Both Kelly and Chloride were mining towns that drew treasure hunters, job seekers and both sets of my grandparents to the New Mexico territory.

In 1866 lead, zinc, smithsonite and silver ore deposits were discovered amid New Mexico's Magdalena Mountains. By 1883, the town of Kelly was established with a post office, banks, churches, saloons, bath houses, a clinic, schools and general stores. Because the Kelly Mine produced vast amounts of lead, zinc, and silver it became the foremost mine in the New Mexico territory during the nineteenth century. The Kelly Mine headframe stands proudly as a tribute to New Mexico's famous mining heritage.

Until approximately 1885 Kelly was plagued by numerous Indian attacks. The town set up railroad cars to carry women and children to safety in nearby Socorro if needed in case of an all-out attack. By 1931 mining had declined and by 1947 the last resident moved away, causing Kelly to spiral into the ghost town that it is today.

In 1879 silver was discovered in Chloride. The area became known as the Apache Mining District with many successful mines operating in the area producing silver ore, copper, lead and zinc.

Chloride boasted saloons, general stores, restaurants, a millinery shop, a butcher shop, hotels, a school, a pharmacy, and even a Chinese laundry. The Black Range newspaper was published in Chloride from approximately 1882 to 1896.

Right from its inception, marauding Indians viciously attacked Chloride. In early 1884 "The territorial Government" gave the residents permission to form their own militia to protect themselves against the attacks. There were 51 volunteers ranging in age from 18-58, some from foreign countries and many came from out of state.

With any reports of Indians in the area the militia would be called up to stand guard on the high ground on both sides of Chloride. If requested they would escort travelers in and out of the area. The militia built a large adobe building to serve as an armory and barracks.

By 1896 the price of silver had plummeted, causing the demise of Chloride. Today, only the St. Cloud Mine remains active in the area, it produces zeolite. It is located approximately two miles east of Chloride with only thirteen residents remaining.

The decline of the mines in other districts forced people to move to Hillsboro and Kingston, where silver and gold were still strong and there was work at the many cattle, sheep and goat ranches surrounding the area.

Hillsboro was the county seat until about 1936

according to some historians, while others say it remained the county seat until 1938. Between Hillsboro and Kingston there was a substantial population, but the exact number remains undetermined.

Ancestry

Dad's a Sephardic Jew and mother is of French, Apache, English and Spanish ancestry. They were both beautiful and handsome. They made a striking couple with dad's Mediterranean good looks and mother's strikingly beautiful black hair and fair skin. She was a beautiful woman. I remember the way mother applied her matte coral lipstick to create round full lips just like the beloved actress Lucille Ball.

Mother said that her father was kind, and that her mother was the instigator of the abuse she and her siblings endured. If she was sent across town to the Hillsboro business district to run errands, upon returning home she'd be accused of carousing with men and would get a beating.

Mother only went through early primary grades in school. She was the oldest of her six siblings (three brothers and three sisters) and had the responsibility of taking care of them. She and her sisters fought a lot when they were older so my guess is that they also fought when they were young.

When I was young I didn't know much about my father or his family since he was out of my life at such an early age. Mother did her best to keep us away from him. I know nothing about his schooling or education. Prior to being drafted during WWII daddy worked at some of the mines that were still in existence in Hillsboro. He wrote in beautiful cursive, dressed impeccably and made a wonderful fashion statement.

Both of my parents lived and met in Hillsboro. They got married at Our Lady of Guadalupe Catholic Church in Hillsboro on September 3, 1938. The original church collapsed after a disastrous flood in 1972. It was rebuilt and currently hosts a monthly Sunday service.

My parents wedding reception took place in a historic twenty-four inch thick walled adobe building right down the street from the church. The building still stands proudly. When it was built in 1877 it was a mercantile; later turned dance hall. It features original floors, tin ceiling and stucco. Dad and mom loved to dance and they celebrated their wedding for two entire days according to some of Hillsboro's long term residents.

It would prove to be a toxic and lethal relationship. Mother came into the marriage with all the baggage that comes from abuse; consequently they fought all the time.

I remember an overstuffed chair in the living room where I'd hide when they'd start fighting. That corner where the chair sat was my "go to" place whenever I got scared. I spent much time there, hiding, hoping to never be found. This is when I'd think "Jesus, please come get me".

After my oldest sister was born at home in Hillsboro my parents moved quite often. I know that they lived in Bayard and Hurley, New Mexico and even Los Angeles, California. They ultimately returned to Hillsboro before I was born. They moved often in search of work, because after World War II there were not many jobs anywhere.

Dad and mother never seemed to find peace together, and ultimately separated and divorced. Their marriage lasted thirteen years. Mother would go on to marry three more times. When she wasn't married she always had boyfriends. Daddy never remarried.

I never believed that mother ever stopped loving daddy; no matter how negatively she spoke of him. Without a doubt he also loved her. Mother was just too wounded and didn't have the skills required to maintain a healthy relationship. Two days after mother passed away I dreamed of the two of them together, young, innocent and in love.

CHAPTER THREE
My Early Years

We lived in a tiny adobe house in Hillsboro that my grandfather built in the late 1920's - a three-room dwelling with no electricity or running water. We would heat water from the well for washing dishes or our washtub baths. The outhouse squatted about forty or fifty feet from the house.

Nobody talks about the poor section of Hillsboro called Happy Flats. I understand that it was given that name because mostly Latinos and Spaniards lived there and they were always happy and joyful. Most of the men worked at the mines or at one of the local ranches. Some families also produced fruit, vegetables and game for the greater Hillsboro community.

My maternal grandparents, their three sons and four daughters lived under a large cottonwood tree in the middle of Percha Creek. It is one of creeks that courses its way through the town of Hillsboro. They cooked over a makeshift griddle outdoors, where the prairie winds would pick up the tortillas or whatever else wasn't weighted down and would send them flying.

My maternal grandfather was a gambler. He earned a fair amount of money and was lucky, but his substantial earnings and wins would return regularly to the poker table and back into the pockets of those he previously won from. Once, when his pockets were empty, he wagered my grandmother, hoping to end a long losing streak. The stakes were high and it was the biggest gamble of his lifetime, but he figured it was time for a win. In one swift game he lost his wife, dignity and respect. I would have loved to be a fly on the wall to observe his gambling demise.

Grandmother raised turkeys to keep food on the table since there were no guarantees that grandpa would return home with any money. After the wager of his lifetime and losing he returned home, sold the turkeys she raised to use the money to buy her back. That undoubtedly started the fight of the century!

My grandfather was gentle, I remember him holding me tenderly and rocking me. He stared into my eyes as though I were a precious jewel. His eyes told me that I was the tiniest, most beautiful creature ever, safe in grandfather's arms. This has been my fondest childhood memory; without a doubt at that place and time I knew that I was loved.

However, there is one snag in this story that I discovered only recently. My husband and I moved to New Mexico on April 17, 2000 along with my daughter Chef Carrie, to open a restaurant. I learned the truth about grandpa at our local cemetery. I was born in 1947 and to my greatest surprise I learned that grandpa had died a year earlier in 1946! I couldn't believe what was written on his gravestone. I researched it and sure enough it was correct.

The Lord had sent an Angel to hold and prepare me.

The memory of being held and rocked in that old chair is still as vivid today as it was when I was tiny and swaddled. Early on I was given wings that would carry me through the tumultuous journey on which I would embark. The gift of love is how I made it through my childhood; I knew for certain that at one time I had been loved.

While my oldest sister Beth called me "Pumpkin" with tenderness and endearment, my mother called me "Fea" (ugly) and "Raton" (rat). As a child I didn't know that she was projecting her self-loathing onto me.

The girls teased me about being our mother's favorite. In truth, I was simply the most compliant one and spent much time alone with her. I was kept close until I was about thirteen years old; unless we were all taken to New Mexico to stay at our grandmother's for a summer or sometimes for the entire school year.

Mother couldn't work with four little girls in tow, so when she needed to earn enough money to move us to Los Angeles she placed us in an orphanage in Las Cruces. The older kids were taken out every morning to help harvest cotton while the younger children stayed behind. We had a horrible infestation of lice. If you've never experienced having pests on any part of your body it is ghastly. The lice were huge as I could pick them off my scalp one after another. The younger children spent most of the morning crying for their older siblings.

Recently I learned from a friend who has participated in "Healing Rooms" that prayer and cursing lice and fleas has actually killed them instantly. We were at a Christian conference and it was suggested that this be done at some of the poorest lice infested villages around the world.

Exodus 8:16 Say unto Aaron, stretch out thy rod, and smite the dust of the land, that it may become lice throughout all the land of Egypt. Psalm 91:6 nor for the pestilence (fleas and lice) that walketh in darkness, KJV.

   The main food that we ate was called "Atole". It is a porridge made from flour, water or milk, a little sugar and sometimes seasoned with a little cinnamon when it was available. It is cooked until it is thick and usually served warm in a cup, it was very comforting. We were also given a cup of warm, half coffee and half milk. Neither my sisters or I remember what our sleeping arrangements were while at the orphanage.

   When I started doing research about the orphanage there wasn't much to go on as most historians of the Southwest weren't aware that a convent and orphanage had even existed in the area. Here is a summary of what I discovered. From 1928 until 1960 the convent was run by the Sisters of Our Lady of Charity of the Good Shepherd. The land was originally purchased by Dr. Winifred E. Garrison, president of New Mexico College of Agriculture and Mechanic Arts, what is now New Mexico State University. The adobe house was designed by visionary architect Henry C. Trost. Over the years it has changed hands and today is once again a lovely pristine private residence which sits on 1.66 acres of beautifully manicured grounds.

   The property features an attached chapel and has several out buildings. When the Sisters first acquired it; they began the daunting and challenging task of making adobe bricks to use for building dormitories and classrooms to house the increasing population of orphans.

The nuns experienced financial difficulties and did whatever tasks they could to stay afloat. In addition to all the hard work in operating the facility, adding dorm rooms and additional structures, they hand embroidered little handkerchiefs which they sold for about ten cents per dozen. Some of their work sits proudly in museums throughout the United States.

I spent much time researching information about the convent in Mesilla Park, New Mexico. There is a great Word Press article that provides insight into its colorful history; titled "Living in the Past" and can be found at: *mythcreant.wordpress.com/2014/05/22.*

CHAPTER FOUR
Floods in Town

During one of the many wet summers that we spent in Hillsboro we have had torrential rain. It was around 1950 or 1951. The rain kept coming and coming with loud crackling thunder and lightning. Even though it was still daylight the sky lit up as though it were on fire. The creek behind the house overflowed and the water came up to the back door. Grandmother's house was about one-hundred and twenty feet from the creek edge on a higher slope. Water is not a respecter of people or property and doesn't care about the space that it invades. It was everywhere.

Suddenly and swiftly a crescendo of water came rushing down the street from west of town. We were petrified. It came down rapidly and within seconds the house was immersed in its own lake. No steps or road could be seen. The house jutted out as though a new island had just been created.

There was no phone to call for help and it seemed as though there was nothing that a grandmother and four frightened girls could do. Grandmother was debating about whether or not to wade across the road to the north side of the street so we could climb the hills to safety, when suddenly she became angry and was now on a mission. As we watched in horror she speedily went into the kitchen and grabbed the largest butcher knife that she could find. She said that she was going to cut the clouds and that is exactly what she did. Grandmother walked out the door and standing in knee deep water said a few words while shaking the huge knife at the sky. To our shock and disbelief it immediately stopped raining.

I don't know why my sisters and I were at home and not at school that day. When the school bus returned from Hot Springs with all the kids on board it couldn't get through all the water. Two local residents who still live in Hillsboro said that their father took his road grader and slowly crossed the water multiple times to retrieve the children off the bus. He would pick up two kids; take them to safety and return to rescue two more. It was nightfall by the time all the children had been rescued and everyone was home safe.

I never did ask grandmother about the knife event and don't know if any of my sisters ever asked her about it. It may have been something she learned from her Apache relatives. We may never know for certain.

CHAPTER FIVE
Johnny's Cafe

When we first arrived in Los Angeles mother worked at Johnny's Café. She would take me with her and I would sit for hours, frozen with terror on the doorstep of the storeroom. Mice crawled everywhere. When mother got off work nothing seemed as bad as having to sit outside that storeroom as I have absolutely no memories once we left her place of work and evening came.

However, that is what I thought until the buried memories started to flood my consciousness. I clearly had no recall of what occurred after we left the cafe. Those evenings were a complete blur.

I should have been accustomed to the mouse problem, because when my parents first divorced, mother took a job in El Paso. We lived in a small abandoned building. At night the floor was covered with mice. To my absolute horror my sister Bonnie took to playing with them. The five of us slept together on maybe a cot or a metal table. I don't remember what it really was that we slept on, only that it was crowded and very uncomfortable.

I started kindergarten in Los Angeles, California. I have only one memory (and a fond one) as a five year old; I had a friend whose name I don't even remember. During recess she and I would hold hands as we walked out to the school yard, we would sit on a bench, and most often neither one of us would say a single word. We would watch the other children play and laugh but never ventured beyond what we perceived as our comfort and safety zone. I know that we were both fearful of life and when together knew that we had found a safe place. In those moments we understood that our bond was sacred and we were protected.

Mother worked as a waitress at Johnny's Café for many years. Her earnings in tips were substantial enough that she saved enough to buy a brand new car and eventually a brand new house. Later she went on to work in various restaurants and blue collar jobs. She wasn't schooled but she was smart.

CHAPTER SIX
Mother Married Joe

I was eight years old when mother got married a second time. Joe appeared to be the love of her life. They loved to dance and spent every weekend out at nightclubs. Mom wore beautiful sequined skirts and blouses. For the first time in many years she was actually happy and was becoming quite pleasant. They got along really well and they couldn't do enough for each other, they were madly and wonderfully in love. They had decided to get married outside the country and it was exciting.

He was kind and seemed to be a great step-father. I liked and trusted him, even felt safe and protected when he was around. What I remember most is that he had a joyful heart. He took time to make me feel good about myself. He encouraged my interest in learning about God and attending catechism. I was happy and would actually skip on my way to class. He made sure that mother had enough money to buy me a special dress and new shoes for my first Holy Communion. In my research I learned that I actually made my communion twice, once in Los Angeles, California and once in New Mexico.

When Disneyland opened in 1955 he took us all and it was the first time that we'd had so much fun. We felt like a family right from the start. We ate good food and returned home with souvenirs.

Unfortunately for all of us the marriage didn't last very long. Mother learned that Joe was already married and had other children. As would be expected, all hell broke loose in our house. That's the first time I'd heard the word bigamy. It became clear why it was important for them to get married outside the United States. It was difficult to understand his commitment elsewhere because he and mother were together from the very first weekend that they met early in 1955. Joe tried to worm his way out of it but there was no turning back. There was no doubt that he loved mother but was already conveniently married. He tried everything he could including a desire to divorce his wife but it was all too late. What Joe never knew was that mother gave birth to his beautiful baby daughter.

It had been the first time in many years that we experienced a glimpse of joy. Along with shattered dreams went my beautiful communion dress and veil. I never understood what happened to them, but after Joe was gone they were nowhere to be found. She probably destroyed any and all reminders of him.

Mother dealt with her grief mostly by speaking about how men could not be trusted. We'd hear over and over how they all cheat. As time went on mother became more bitter eventually returning to her old self.

CHAPTER SEVEN
Mother Pregnant

After we moved to California we would return and spend our summers and sometimes the entire school year in New Mexico with our maternal grandmother. In 1955 we arrived in June and stayed through part of the school year. I was eight years old. Mother and Joe had just split up and I remember clearly she was overly anxious to drop us off and return to Los Angeles.

I attended the one room schoolhouse up on the hill in our little village. There probably weren't more than ten of us in that old schoolhouse. The older children were bussed to a school in Hot Springs about thirty-five miles away.

When my sisters got on that school bus every morning it was pretty daunting. I was scared as I walked alone to school. When the creek bed was dry there were always rattlesnakes in and around the mesquite bushes. If the creek was running I couldn't get across because there were no bridges.

Unbeknown to my sisters and me, our mother was pregnant when she dropped us off at grandmas that summer. Because she was recently unmarried it was a disgrace to be with child. She was only a few months pregnant so it didn't take any effort to disguise her pregnancy.

Mom had already made plans to place the child up for adoption. She returned to Los Angeles and gave birth to a healthy baby girl in November and she never looked back. She completely closed that chapter in her life. My sisters were older and should have been more astute, but we were all programmed and controlled not to have our own thoughts.

In earlier times most adoptions in California were arranged through the hospitals whereas in New Mexico adoptions were handled through the Catholic Diocese.

CHAPTER EIGHT
1956 Stinking Drunk

After we had spent the entire summer in New Mexico mother came to pick us up to take us back to California in time to start school.

Grandmother was a heavy drinker and the night before we were to leave she brought out her bottle of tequila. All the adults proceeded to drink and get highly intoxicated. My grandma wanted me to have a drink. She never liked me so I thought that would be a way to ingratiate myself to her. I took one drink but she insisted that I keep drinking and no one came to my defense. I fell into a near comatose state. We weren't able to leave for several days as I drifted in and out of consciousness and didn't care if I lived or died.

I acquired an aversion toward alcohol and still not much of a fan. I didn't take my next drink until my twenty-fourth birthday at a work celebration. I cook with it, especially with rum and I enjoy plum wine with Japanese food but can't even be considered a social drinker.

For most of my life I knew that grandmother didn't like me. I also had the grim realization that mom didn't like me either. I choked back tears and reasoned that what I felt couldn't be true. They had to love me I was their daughter and granddaughter. I was a model child probably out of fear, but good I was.

After grandmother's death mother admitted, the truth that grandmother had never liked me. It's something I always knew; children are more tuned in and sometimes as adults we start doubting ourselves about what we know. I know that mine and grandmother's differences stemmed, because our spirits clashed.

People are controlled by voices that they aren't aware of and grandmother was being influenced by those. There are three voices in our mind that are always talking; ours, the Enemy and the Lord's. We must learn to discern the differences so that the enemy cannot influence us. If you have any doubt about whose voice it is check the scriptures because the enemy's voice will never match with the word of God.

```
2 Corinthians 10:5 (NIV) ········ and we take
captive every thought to make it obedient to
Christ.
```

The enemy knew I was determined to break the chains of generational bondage. My journey has been long and arduous. I was born for this. My prayer is that the Lord uses me to fulfill his purpose, because that is the reason that I was created in the first place.

I know we have a big loving God and he sent his only Son to set us free. The moment Jesus was nailed to that wooden cross he took all our iniquities and infirmities with him. Today I am free and no longer a victim; although our journey never ends until we are united with him who created us.

Mother moved us to California to get away from her family. Her thoughts were that by moving us we'd have a better life. What she didn't take into account was that she'd need to heal herself first in order to improve our lives. She knew that her family was toxic but didn't acknowledge the role she played contributing to that toxicity.

The family on mother's side is pretty noxious. Her three sisters and two of her brothers had many issues. There were innumerable kinds of abuse perpetrated by them onto their children.

Mother was always in control and that goes hand in hand with fear. That is a curse that causes you to acquire disease and it is passed down through the blood line. Most if not all of my mother's sisters died of some form of cancer.

One uncle was kind and loving and was always good to his children. He was a good husband and father but he suffered a terrible accident in a mine shaft. During an explosion he was thrown and was blinded. His work days were over but he never became bitter or mean.

Steve and I recently completed a couple of studies, one by Dr. Carolyn Leaf, a neuroscientist. One of her best sellers is titled "Who Switched off My Brain"? It is about controlling toxic thoughts and emotions. Another great book is titled "A More Excellent Way" by Dr. Henry W. Wright. Because I understand the nature of disease I have a responsibility to do something about it. These curses will not be passed on to my children or my sister's children. Period!

CHAPTER NINE
Toys, what toys?

A friend of mother gave me my first doll when I was nine years old. I was so excited and devoted to this strawberry blond haired doll with the Marilyn Monroe bob. My doll arrived carefully packed inside her red a white checkered suitcase. I made all her clothes from material scraps and fussed over her every chance I got.

We never had toys so this doll meant the world to me. I loved her but unfortunately only had her for a short time as one day she disappeared along with her travel case never to be seen again. I cried privately and silently for days. I don't remember ever having another toy. None of us had much. I remember one of my sisters checking out a doll from our local library when we lived in Los Angeles, because back then you could actually check out toys.

After losing the things that I loved I could not accept gifts until I was about 24 years old. If something came from my sisters I made an exception. But still, I would not get attached; if I did the item would mysteriously disappear. Material things mean very little to me. I know that items were taken from me as a way of punishment but I never understood the reason behind it.

CHAPTER TEN
Beth's Wedding

The same year that I received my pink haired doll, my oldest sister Beth got married. She had met her boyfriend the last year that we attended school in New Mexico. After he graduated from high school he joined the United States Navy and was stationed in San Diego. We lived in Los Angeles at the time so he was close enough that he was able to visit her on weekends. Shortly after arriving in San Diego he proposed and they got married.

I loved Beth so much, but it was her time and opportunity to move out of our dysfunctional home. She was my savior and protector, I mourned her as if she had died. She always made sure that my shoes were polished and that my clothes were laundered. She combed my hair every morning.

When her first son was born I felt a resentment that was new to me. I didn't know what to do with such uncomfortable feelings, as Beth no longer had time for me and I felt totally lost.

When Beth's husband was called to go on tour she invited me to spend time with her and my nephew over the summer. I was elated, it was perfect. I didn't realize at the time that it was the beginning of climactic changes for my life.

CHAPTER ELEVEN
Unworthy

My reluctance to write this story is that there are millions throughout the world that have faced abuse of one kind or another. Is this story any different and how could it help anyone? There are thousands of self-help books lining shelves at store's and libraries, but it was the influence by my Sozo Minister. He believed I was different, because I used no crutches to ease the pain, no drugs, alcohol or sexual release. I learned to push through pain and discomfort and at times I just escaped into my benign fantasy world.

I don't want pity or sympathy nor do I wish to hurt my sisters who are still in their own denial and choose only to half live than to live in truth. I call their world never, never land as I believe they are only partly awake.

My story is a topic that no one ever talks about; my goal is that it will help someone that has traveled in my footsteps to know that they aren't alone, that they aren't crazy or fear that no one will believe that these things happen.

During high school drugs were rampant, but when they were present I'd get away as fast as possible. There was no way that I would try ingesting or doing something that could ultimately control me more than I'd been already.

Where do I start with the adjectives mother used to refer to me; pinche (scullion), puta (bitch or whore), pendeja (stupid), you'll never amount to anything.

Early in life my fundamental belief was established that no matter what I did I wasn't good enough, I was still ugly according to mother and felt as insecure as a lost puppy.

See, when I was never invited to a prom or homecoming dance I considered myself to be that ugly duckling. It would be at my ten year reunion before I would really understand why I wasn't considered a propitious partner. No one asked me because they thought I was aloof and they feared rejection. Insecurity or low self-esteem can be easily clouded by appearing aloof.

I didn't understand the frequency of the nosebleeds that I would get. It would be years later before I understood the power of the soul; and my soul was dying. Somehow my desire to live was greater than the desire to die. I thought there would no one to come to my rescue and that I was on my own. I didn't always acknowledge it, but knew that my Savior Jesus Christ was always there to help and save me from pain and the bad memories that were stored in cells throughout my body.

My safety net was the hospital, which I loved escaping to. There I was treated with loving tenderness. Bouts of pneumonia and tonsillitis were guaranteed entrance to the hospital. Hernia, appendicitis and a broken arm meant a good long hospital stay.

But the nosebleeds, they were out of my control. Doctors tried everything to stop them but with very little success. Forceps pushed vast amounts of cotton wadding up my nostrils. It was extremely painful as different methods were tried.

After I started menstruating I might hemorrhage from the nostrils or vaginally. Doctors were amazed at the amount of blood that I could lose and recover on my own.

Beth tells me that whenever I hemorrhaged I would ask her

"if I died would I become an angel"?

I guess that I didn't have a concept that our Lord had already created angelic beings.

CHAPTER TWELVE
Middle School

In spite of the turmoil in my life, in many aspects I was successful. In Middle school I learned and accomplished many things that delighted and intrigued me. We had a gifted home economics teacher and because of her, I became fond of different foods and learned to appreciate methodology of cooking. One of the first dishes we mastered in home economics was Eggplant Parmesan. It has remained a classic in our home and is one of my favorite entrees. Can you imagine mastering such an elegant dish in middle school home economics. Today they don't even offer such basic courses. I think our kids are missing out on some real practical skills.

I also mastered my sewing and design skills. We were given a challenge to make a beautiful dress from our own creative ability. I purchased pink and white seersucker material and a yard of lovely cotton eyelet lace. I decorated the neck edge and the end of three quarter sleeves with the lace. It turned out perfect. I received honorable mention and got to place my dress in the junior high fashion show, it was very exciting. It was the prettiest dress that I ever owned; but I was heartbroken because like other special things in my life it also vanished.

That summer I got my first real job at a clothing

factory, doing something other than babysitting. I was thirteen years old and a neighbor of ours helped me get hired. Of course I lied about my age and I passed for a sixteen year old. We were paid by piecework and the newcomer got the work that was most disdained. They got the parts of the garment that nobody wanted. As a result, I can set sleeves and zippers practically with my eyes closed. Today that is an employable skill if you live in a third world country.

A couple of days before middle school graduation I came home from school so ill that I could barely walk. I went right to bed. The pain in my stomach was so excruciating that I thought I would die right there alone in my bed.

A few hours later mother came home from work. "What's wrong with you, are you having a bad day?" She had a guest with her and didn't want to be troubled.

I lay there for hours hunched over and crying. She finally came in and asked if I needed to go to the hospital. It was close to 10 pm when we arrived at the emergency room. Jesus was definitely watching over me. My appendix was close to rupturing.

I don't remember much else about that day except waking up the following morning in a bed in the hospital corridor and felt as though a twenty pound weight was on my abdomen. Outpatient surgery was uncommon so I had a nice long hospital stay. I remember the kind nurses coming in to check on me; how did I feel or was I hungry. They'd bring me ice cream, Jell-O and other treats, and I never wanted to leave.

I was disappointed that I missed my middle school

graduation but thoroughly enjoyed my hospital visit. I had no one that would have attended my graduation anyway.

Again the following year I came home from school with an awful pain and discomfort on the same side as the appendicitis. It wasn't as severe but pretty awful. I had no clue what it was and suspected that the pain was related to the previous year's problem.

I ended up back in the hospital emergency room. I needed immediate surgery for a hernia. It was a rather large tear and because it sat right above my right ovary I was told that I might have trouble conceiving when I got married. God knew better and I have been blessed with three super neat children. The hospital was always good for several days away from home. I loved the pampering, love and even the gifts of candy and comic books.

By the time I turned fourteen I was hired as an apprentice to an Italian designer. I was soon creating and sewing custom designed fashions. During school, I worked part time and throughout the summer at Anmar Fashions. Anna was an Italian designer and her husband Mario handled the business tasks. Both Anna and Mario hadn't been in America very long and both spoke broken English with a heavy accent.

They were kind, smart and willingly taught me and generously shared their trade secrets of the garment industry. They took me under their wings as they had no children of their own. I was an eager and fast learner. Even though I only had my red haired doll for a short while I had spent many months creating "fashions" for her. I was a designer.

Mother drove me to work for a while because whatever

paycheck we earned was "cheerfully" signed over to her. When she didn't want to drive me anymore I had to quit as I couldn't get a ride. It was at a neighboring city and bus transportation wasn't available.

My skills are natural talent that I was born with, otherwise how I could have accomplished what I have been able to do. When God created us before time began he made each of us distinct with our own characteristics and abilities. When we aren't connected with what our Lord destined for us we might feel a sense of frustration that we don't understand.

We go through life with a deep yearning and a void that can't be filled.

```
Psalm 139:16 Your eyes saw my unformed body. All
the days ordained for me were written in your book
before one of them came to be. NIV
```

CHAPTER THIRTEEN
Angel in the car

Two of my best friends were also from broken homes. We were all Catholic. Terry came from a large Irish family with three brothers and four sisters. When we were in high school, our local Irish priest visited Terry's family regularly. Terry hated it but I never understood why she detested his visits. I learned later that according to her mother it was alright if the priest "man handled" all the girls in the family. After all, he was a man of the cloth. God help us as this is another example of depriving children of their innocence and purity. The reverence that we have for our clergy is sometimes nauseating as they are human just like us and sins of the flesh are no less a sin for them.

My friends would tease me that no matter what went wrong in their lives if they thought about me they knew that I must be praying on their behalf. "Not really" was my response. We were kids and I was probably praying supernaturally at a level I wasn't even aware of. We didn't have a bible in our home so the essence of his word didn't come alive with the weightiness that it carries until recently.

There was an incident that my friends and I will never forget. Mother was overly strict with me never permitting me to go to parties or dances. I could have girlfriends spend the night but we weren't allowed to leave the house, on some occasions we did sneak out. Mother owned her restaurant during my high school years; consequently she was gone long hours. One particular evening we wanted to attend a church dance in a neighboring town about thirty-five miles away.

My friend's parents were always willing to drive us wherever we wanted to go. There were four of us wanting to attend the dance, the friend that was spending the night and two sisters who lived a few houses away on the same street. One parent took us but in our excitement we didn't arrange for a pick-up.

The dance ended and by the time we realized our mistake, we stood all alone outside the rear entrance of a vacant building looking at an empty parking lot. No one could see us from the street and we had no way to call for help. We were petrified. It was pitch black and not a soul in sight. I started praying, maybe we all did, a few hours had passed when a car turned the corner and drove right up to us. It was a funny little car the likes of which we'd never seen before; a small cream colored, square looking four door sedan like the smaller, square looking cars that you see in third world countries.

The driver was large, not fat just a really big man, he looked like a giant in a mini car. He said four words, "you need a ride". Normally the thought of riding with a stranger is frightening but we had no fear, a little concern but no fear. We willfully got into the car and strategized about which pair of us would be dropped off first. Other than that not a word was said by us or our driver and he seemed to know exactly where we lived. He drove right up to the first driveway then all four of us decided to get out since we lived on the same street. We thanked him and thanked God for sending us someone to take us home safely.

I was more frightened about getting in trouble but we still arrived home before mother and didn't get caught. My friends were as afraid of mother as I was.

I'm still amazed that God loves us and cares for us even when we are doing something wrong and dishonest. The impression that that incident has had on my life is beyond comprehension. God sent us an angel, it's unbelievable.

CHAPTER FOURTEEN
My Eighteen Year Plan

I had this fantasy that as soon as I turned eighteen I would get in touch with my father. I was 18 years old when we received a call from an uncle, my dad's brother, whom we knew of but I don't recall ever meeting. He spoke with mom and told her that our dad had suffered a fall and was in a coma. For the first time ever, she let us go to him.

We arrived at the hospital to find him stretched out on a bed with his head bandaged. He looked peaceful as though he were sleeping. We spoke to him but of course there was no response; I knew that he could hear my voice. I told him how much I loved him and he died a couple of days later.

At first I was angry at him, real angry. How could he do this to me? I waited all these years, waiting to be rescued, even to run away with him and now he was gone? Overnight those dreams of escape died along with him; I was left crushed and depressed.

It was tough in the 1960's with the drug craze, the hippies, the free love movement and I wanted no part of it. My circle of friends was shrinking as more and more would fall victim to the obscene culture. I desperately needed help and needed to talk to someone, an adult that would listen and care. I didn't have anyone to go to so I approached my high school counselor. I met with Mrs. Fritz, but before I could say anything the first thing she asked "are you pregnant"? With that attitude she couldn't be of any help. What I needed was a caring and compassionate individual. I had too much baggage and needed therapy but didn't have the resources. Because of the obvious dysfunction at home I was aware that my life was messed up but didn't have the faintest idea of all that it really meant or what if anything could be done about it.

At my father's funeral I was informed that I could attend college on his GI bill. Mother wouldn't hear of it as she said that I was too stupid to go to college.

Mother had opened her own restaurant and was successful from the beginning because her food was really great. Unfortunately she started drinking heavily. My sister Bonnie worked for her and sometimes they would both return home inebriated. I hated it and never knew what to expect and I didn't want to be around. I needed a reprieve, so shortly after daddy passed away I went and stayed with Bibiana and her husband for a few months. Her sister-in-law also stayed with them so it was pretty cool to have someone to hang out with. I was happy to have a place to go to and mother was happy to see me go.

When I turned eighteen, my future in-laws gave me my first birthday party ever. They invited my mother but she didn't come. My sister Bibiana went shopping and got me a gift and said that it was from our mother, it was all for show as our birthdays were never acknowledged or celebrated. I think I was incensed more than anything as my sisters continued to cover up for mothers lack of caring.

After graduating from high school jobs were plentiful as we were in the middle of the war in Viet Nam. I was able to find a great job at an aeronautics company that produced parts for the M16 rifle. I was hired as a quality control assistant. The quality control manager was a wonderful man to work for and he and his wife exhibited a divine marital relationship. I loved my work but unfortunately, quit because there truly was a lot of sexual harassment as all the inspectors thought that all the young women were fair game. Human resources were more concerned about the government contracts than the welfare of the employees.

Working and doing well financially I would have loved to move out and be on my own, but mother wouldn't have permitted it. She was still totally in control of my life.

CHAPTER FIFTEEN
My Wedding

Just before my twentieth birthday mother did something extraordinary. She called me to the living room and told me to kneel down. I didn't know what to expect but then she proceeds to bless me. Keep in mind that she wasn't kind so that came as a total shock. To this day I still don't understand that contradiction in her demeanor.

Mother was particularly strict with me. I wasn't allowed to date but John charmed his way into her life. He'd stop by even when I wasn't at home and lavish her with a box of chocolates or some other memento.

He eventually won her over and I have to say being a teenager I was pretty excited to go on a date. I was twenty years old when John and I got married on September 2, 1967, while he was in the military. We had a small church wedding at Epiphany Catholic Church, in South El Monte, (a suburb North-East of Los Angeles), and a reception was held at the home of my sister Beth and her husband.

John was stationed at Fort Ord, California. Fort Ord Army Base closed in 1994 but it had been the most beautiful Army base in the United States as it was in Monterey Bay on the Pacific Ocean coast. John only had a weekend pass so we left our reception early to catch a flight the same day. As soon as we arrived at the base housing I got terribly ill. I vomited and vomited and went to sick bay. After a visit to the base medic, John's commanding officer gave him permission to fly me back home. It was a combination of things that had made me ill.

I'd grown up in a household filled with women. I'd never had sex and I'd never seen a penis in my entire life except on my nephew when he was born. I'd never traveled except to my childhood home. Everything was new to me and I was terrified. I recovered quickly as soon as I got on the plane to return home.

However fearful, I was ecstatic that I'd get to move out of my childhood home. I worked hard and was very resourceful when it came to finances and responsibility so I could handle the obligation of paying rent and living on my own. The idea of living on my own was like a dream come true even if it would be temporary. Then came the next blow and I was crushed. Mother and John's parents decided that I would live with them until John returned from the military. I went from one oppressive controlling home to another.

Because of my early training to work hard as an expression of my worth it was easy to lose myself in work. I had my full time day job and then I took a night job as well as it was easy to get night work at the local drive-in theatre. I worked from dusk to about two am five days a week.

Working kept me busy and I didn't have to spend every evening with my in-laws. I didn't realize then that as my in-laws required more and more help from me, I was being groomed to be the servant daughter-in-law for their son when he would return from Viet Nam.

When John returned from Viet Nam he came home a different man. At times he was secretive and easily got his feathers ruffled. In my mind I was back home living with my mother.

We saved enough money to purchase our first home a year after he got out of the military. I started community college to obtain my basic credits but, since I was working full time and commuting to work created an eleven hour day, I was only able to handle two classes. By my second semester I was registering with a baby in my arms. I studied psychology and sociology thinking that I'd pursue a degree in psychology.

There was so much going on in my life that I made the decision to put college on hold. During the following years I did a little interior design work and my husband and I opened a German import store. We specialized in music boxes and hand-painted imports. We worked closely with a minister that would smuggle bibles in suitcases into East Germany and bring back hand made collectibles that we sold in our shop.

For the first time in my life I was exploring and discovering that I had many diverse interests. I took an interest and ability assessment test and discovered not to my surprise that my strongest ability was in the design field. Not just in the creative world of clothing or interior but an ability to design in the technical arena. To weed out my diverse interests I studied technical design and became certified to design power drives, conveyor belts and anything that had to do with automation primarily designated for food industry. Automation was fascinating but it didn't hold my interest.

In the interim I studied various subjects but I didn't return to college full time until I was in my early forties. I studied Fashion Design and maintained a 3.9975 GPA. I don't think I ever believed that I was stupid as mother said that I was.

After John and I married we attended St. John Vianney Roman Catholic Church in Southern California. Father O'Callahan was a gentle giant with a heart for God. The church had a very large membership and our church family was great.

We were the first church in Southern California that recognized the need to teach teenagers in a home setting. They were starting to lose interest and were restless in a staunch classroom environment. The state of Michigan was a forerunner in new church teachings and doctrine. They had success teaching catechism to teen's at home so we took our lead from them.

I was blessed to offer the first probationary teen class at home. It was a huge success. I also taught early catechism to three and four year olds; what an awesome experience that turned out to be. During our first semester one of our four year olds passed away over a weekend. My teaching partner and I didn't know how we were going to tell the other children that one of their friends would no longer be in class. They were all close but to our surprise were excited, giggled and joyfully expressed that their friend was lucky because he had gone to live with Jesus. Children are filled with insight and wonder.

In the early 1970's St. John Vianney was a charismatic

church filled with the Holy Spirit. The gift of tongues was prolific. At our prayer meetings the sound of prayer was heavenly like the wind blowing a gentle breeze through a cluster of trees. Like what you hear as Angels fly when their wings flutter.

I attended bible study and prayer services taught by a wonderful spirit- filled teacher by the name of Kay. She was the first of many Godly women that would influence my life and had a tender heart for Christ and was an amazing teacher.

I remember one of our early studies was from the Book of Luke. The most memorable scripture was Luke 4:18, about setting the captives free. It is a one that resonates with me. I had lived my life as a prisoner. Some freely volunteer to be victims but children don't have a choice.

CHAPTER SIXTEEN
My Son Armando

In the summer of 1969 I started to get really sick. I couldn't eat and spent much time with an upset stomach vomiting. I took my pillow and laid a blanket down on the bathroom floor because sometimes I couldn't get there fast enough. I'd vomit until the dry heaves started and then I'd have to go to the hospital to get an injection to calm the heaving. Neither I nor my doctor suspected that I could be pregnant because my periods continued as before.

After a few months my doctor decided to do a pregnancy test not because he suspected that I might be but because nothing else was showing up. The test came back positive. I was elated but remained chronically ill and my periods continued for a few more months.

When I was six months pregnant I came in contact with someone with German measles. I knew what the possible implications were for contact of this type. I called Dr. Gallager, my gynecologist and told him what had happened. He arranged an immediate appointment to have some test's run. I was nervous while I waited for the results but kept up with my prayers that the outcome would be good. The day arrived for the results. I fidgeted nervously in the waiting room but as soon as my doctor walked in I knew the answer as the first thing he said was that he would arrange travel for me to go to Arizona.

He said that since both I and my child came back positive for German measles that I would need an abortion. It would have to be expedient since I was so far along. He continued that abortion wasn't yet "legal" in California but he had a colleague in Arizona that would take care of it. I was flabbergasted; he didn't ask, but assumed that I would do any such thing. I've been blessed to even be pregnant especially when you consider that I had been told that I might not ever be able to conceive.

He went on to "highlight" everything that could go wrong. I looked at him and straight away said in no uncertain terms "NO". If God the creator wants this child let him take it from me. Not some doctor that doesn't honor his oath of saving life.

Declaration of Geneva of the World Medical Association states "I will maintain the utmost respect for human life from its beginning even under threat and I will not use my medical knowledge contrary to the laws of humanity".

By the time I delivered a perfect, healthy six pound son I had lost forty pounds. I looked like a straw that had swallowed a large grape. I started to believe that the enemy did not want my son to be born. Things would happen to him that didn't make any sense like when he lost sight in one eye and doctors could provide no explanation for the loss. All they could do was patch his good eye and hope that it would force restoration of sight in the almost blind eye. He wore powerful eye glasses so he could see a little with his poor eye. I told him what a fine little pirate he was.

A lovely priest that I knew well brought over a blessed crucifix from the Vatican and suggested we place it under his mattress where his head lies. His lost sight was completely restored in a relative short amount of time.

My son Armando is a kind, gentle loving human being and really smart. He could read from about the age of three (before they patched his good eye) and he would read me a bedtime story. He was a gracious little host whenever someone came over. He'd offer everyone coffee no matter how old they were.

In 1978 the smoke of Satan entered our parish. Our church brought in a visiting sect of brothers from the archdiocese. Our pastor was a godly man and didn't see the evil as it permeated slowly. Armando would fall victim to the whim of one of those perverted brothers. According to my son he was excused to go to the restroom. He didn't think much about it when he was followed by a visiting brother.

My eight year old said that he was raped inside the boy's bathroom. I can't even fathom how terrified my little boy must have been. His life was threatened, that of his six year old brother (who was also at catechism) and that of his parents if he ever told anyone of the incident. He was just a child preparing for a holy sacrament. He has lived with this terror his whole life.

Prior to this horrific event he played soccer on the same team with his brother and they were inseparable. Afterwards we'd look at photographs of him and knew that something had happened, his joy was gone and it seemed that his spirit was crushed. His dad was awfully strict, at times was verbally and emotionally abusive so I thought that was what shattered him.

We were certain that whatever had happened to him was catastrophic. We'd ask question but he would give no response. He was about thirteen years old when he started smoking pot. I was naïve as I'd never been around anyone who did any kind of drugs. My girlfriend, a psychiatric nurse, was visiting and called it to my attention. I made the decision to put him in rehab in California hoping that he could turn his life around.

One day while visiting him in rehab he said "mom quit wasting your money, if we want drugs we can get them in here. Besides I can out-smart all the psychiatrists". He is super intelligent and he was absolutely correct. After a few months and at a cost of approximately $87,000.00 I took him home as I didn't feel that we were getting anywhere with the treatments.

The only good thing that came out of that first confinement was that through testing we learned that he was not only smart but a super genius the likes of Mensa.

From about the time Armando turned thirteen our lives were like riding a roller coaster twenty-four seven. It would be another twenty-eight years before he was able to get past the fear and the shame that was on him because of someone else's sin and confess to us what had happened to him that dreadful day.

The sin of sex and fear that entered in him the day of the rape was the catalyst to a long life of drugs, alcohol and sexual immorality. Today he is lost but we know that God's word is true, he doesn't lie, and he finds all his lost sheep. He will bring back our son in the image of his own Son, Jesus Christ.

Seemingly innocuous things would continue to happen to him. One time he came in contact with poison ivy. He got so sick; we made trips back and forth to the hospital. His entire system externally and internally had become poisoned. He blew up like Popeye to the point that his skin was about to burst. Eventually the hospital sent him home saying that there was nothing more they could do for him. They had given him every known drug used to treat poison ivy and nothing worked. I took him home, prayed and prayed. We were very grateful that he gradually improved. He had missed so much school by the time he was healed. It's a good thing that he was smart, so missing school didn't affect him.

One evening when he was living with his employer he called Steve and me. He was alone and terrified, he said please pray for me right now. I'm surrounded by demons. The moment we started praying I had a vision of him and it was definitely evil. He was in his bed surrounded by dark creepy figures depicting themselves as angels. They formed a complete circle around his bed as though they were keeping something out. We continued to pray until the vision ceased and he felt at peace.

I cried and prayed constantly as the pain of a Prodigal child is unbearable. You are always asking yourself what you could have done differently. How could I have been a better parent and the constant blame that you place on yourself is heart wrenching.

We rescued him more times than I can count. Not until we realized that we were co-dependent were we able to completely release him back to God. We find peace knowing that our Father in Heaven loves him so much more than we ever could. In 1997 Armando wrote the following poem while in rehab when he lived in Mammoth Lakes, California.

"This is where the end begins,
where we begin to pay for our sins.
When all we've done was lived and loved.
Our dreams fly away just like a dove.
Maybe it's because the way we made our living,
that now our sorry soul must now start giving.
It's always harder for others than for you,
because, you've lost all your worries and they've lost you.
This is when they are reminded in that all too familiar way,
that you'll all be together hopefully someday".

We truly believe that God has a master plan for our son's life. Whatever is written in his book in Heaven will be nothing short of extraordinary.

CHAPTER SEVENTEEN
Therapy 1971

After John returned from Viet Nam he had outbursts of unpredictable screaming. He was also having really bad nightmares. This escalated after our son was born. He became easily agitated and had more angry outbursts than before. The stress of a baby seemed to take him over the top. His work schedule changed weekly which may have contributed to his stress and home had become a nightmare.

I needed help and started therapy. It was evident that for the marriage to succeed it would take both of us putting in effort. He wouldn't hear of it as he didn't think that we needed any help, for him everything was as it should be.

When I started therapy in 1971 I was pregnant with my second child, and feeling much trepidation. I knew that ultimately I'd outgrow my marriage, and it would mean that I'd have to confront some issues and make some tough decisions which were contrary to my moral beliefs and fantasy that marriage is wonderful and should last forever, period. After only a few sessions I quit therapy as I wasn't ready to make serious changes for fear of the consequences.

I grew up with so much abuse that I knew how to walk

on eggshells and not rock the boat. My son did not and I would do whatever I needed to do to protect him. The first time John physically abused my son, I drew the line. He was barely eighteen months; I spoke up and stated that I would not tolerate that. He made no effort to change although I'd threatened to leave him. He didn't believe me since I'd never requested anything in my life before so I took up the matter with the person who headed our household; I went to my father-in-law, certainly not out of respect but out of desperation. Also, Armando was his only grandchild and was the love of his life. It did make a difference as he spoke with his son and my son was physically safe but to our dismay the yelling and screaming did not stop.

I continued to be a dedicated wife and mother but in actuality I was so insecure that I was no more than a doormat for my spouse and his parents. I measured my self- worth on how much I did for others, how good I did it and I couldn't do enough for my husband and in-laws. The more I did the more they demanded. Our home was run by my father-in-law, husband and mother-in-law, in that order. I made no requests and was totally discounted as a person.

On one occasion I'd gone in for out-patient surgery, once again to stop bleeding. I returned home to find my mother-in-law there. She was preparing to go on a trip to Spain. I just wanted to go to bed but John demanded that I fix "mother's" hair so she could go catch her flight. It felt as though he'd taken a knife and cut open my heart. On the inside I prayed as I'd done most of my life "please God take me". I am eternally grateful that God did not answer my prayer.

I wanted a second child, first as a companion to my son and also because I loved children. I did conceive but as my pregnancy progressed I grew more and more tired. As first I blamed it on being with child.

My in-laws continued to join us for dinner three to four times a week. My mother-in-law showed up once a week with her best friend, and I was required to prepare lunch for them. Physically I grew wearier. I realized how much energy one exerts living a lie, I was miserable and couldn't find my voice or wherewithal to make changes. As my physical state deteriorated my death wish returned. Only I made one addition to my prayer; that the Lord would take me, my son and my unborn child.

The selfishness in my husband and his family was nauseating; I felt that I couldn't go on. I understood why mother allowed me to date John in the first place as he was just like her. I justified my own selfishness for not wanting to leave my children behind.

For a long time I carried the guilt of breaking up my family. I strived to communicate with John as I desired growth and wholeness for him as well. When I opened up to him his facial expression caused me to withdraw, he couldn't handle it and appeared to be in as much pain as I. His own account of childhood was that everything had always been perfect and happy, while his sister has much different memories and stories about their background.

In therapy I'd hoped for an answer regarding this recurring vision. I'm fighting off someone, my tiny fists are hitting and skinny little arms are swinging, flailing at this invisible faceless attacker but I am always overcome.

I thought that God was telling me that if I was ever attacked that I wouldn't be able to protect myself because I'm small and helpless. This made me more fearful of everything, more than I already was. This is not how God work's, he doesn't give visions of defeat; he gives us successes and answers. This was the work of the enemy.

CHAPTER EIGHTEEN
Christiaan

Christiaan was born in 1972 and he is most definitely our strong willed child determined that no matter what emotional trauma he was put through he was tough and thought that nothing would or could affect him. Christiaan is charismatic and charming. When he was little I was his savior and he always clung to me.

I kept all my kids in private Christian schools as long as I could. Christiaan was always the entrepreneur; starting as early as Kindergarten. He saved his money and everything else that he considered had value and would line up all his little treasures on top of his dresser. One day the principle called me to say that though he appreciates an entrepreneurial spirit that he'd rather Christiaan didn't sell gum and candy at school as it was distracting to say the least.

When I could no longer afford private schooling I transferred him and his brother to public high school. All had many friends in the area so it wasn't a dramatic change as far as making friends; what they didn't like was that they were advanced for their grade and Christiaan complained that his teachers were far too liberal. He said he knew when he was being lied to or mislead. He finished school one year early because he didn't want to deal with the public school system.

Because of his strong will he was always eager to accomplish everything quickly like obtaining a Bachelor's degree in Telecommunications in only three years. Upon graduation he received multiple job offers including an invitation to work at Cape Canaveral. He turned it down because he couldn't bear to leave his very handsome red nose Pit-bull named Duke.

He has various black belts in different styles of martial arts. I think he was seventeen or eighteen when he hired himself two personal trainers to prepare him to compete in 1992 Olympics in the category of martial arts. He did that for a year or so and then decided to do something else. He went on to study acting and even studied at the Royal Academy in London before changing direction again.

Christiaan is also spiritually gifted. One night he came running upstairs to our room. He said "Steve, did you call me?" we replied that we had not. We told him to go back to bed. A second time he comes running upstairs to our room "did you guys call me", again our reply was that we did not call you. Go back to bed and go to sleep. When he came up the third time and said, "I know that you two are calling me," I finally got it and said that when you hear the voice calling again, stay in bed and reply, "yes Lord, your servant is listening." The next time he was called he said "yes Lord, your servant is listening," he looked out toward his open French doors and there stood a large Angel blocking the screened entrance. I'm mesmerized by the awesomeness if God.

Most importantly are that Christiaan and his wife

Barbara are amazing parents to their three super neat children. They are home schooled and are being raised in a Godly home.

Carrie

CHAPTER NINETEEN
Our Princess

I had a period that lasted an entire year and during that time my gynecologist insisted that I have a hysterectomy. I wouldn't hear of it as I knew and believed in my heart that I was to have one more child. I agreed to take medication to stop the bleeding long enough to get pregnant although doctors said that I wouldn't ever conceive again; they were wrong as within one month I did get pregnant.

Our beautiful princess Carrie was born via caesarian but she was perfect and healthy. I always had a desire in my heart to adopt a Chinese baby and as our Lord always comes through, Carrie was born with the most beautiful rice paper complexion and shiny, jet black hair. The only haircut that worked for her was a stunning rice bowl style. She was a a doll and a charmer. Wherever we went she was spotted, with cameras clicking photo's of her.

While I nursed her she stayed healthy but after that she would get one ear infection after another or a throat infection. I didn't understand allergies like I do today and all dairy played havoc in her system. Pediatricians put her on antibiotics repeatedly to no avail.

She was a very precocious little girl. In public she was the perfect little Angel but sometimes at home she could be a little terror partly because we spoiled her like crazy.

My friends John and Sandy operated a Christian pre-school right across the street from where I had my store so it worked out perfectly. I would arrive at my store and just walk Carrie across the street to start my day and hers.

It was probably there that she acquired her love of food and cooking. If they had peanut butter cookies they made them from scratch and if they were having orange juice they had to squeeze their own oranges.

That pre-school system was perfectly set up and orchestrated. I'm certain that the children that attended there have been blessed by the lessons they learned about being self-sufficient. These life skills will be remembered.

Like Christiaan, Carrie was young when she graduated from high school. She initially wanted to be a beautician and studied cosmetology for a while but changed her mind and said that it wasn't what she wanted to do. She apologized to Steve and me for not really knowing what to do with her life and that she didn't want to waste our money. We replied "you're only seventeen most people don't know what they want to do until they're much older." We did tease her about being a beauty school drop-out.

Carrie is naturally gifted in many areas. The next thing she wanted to work in was the design field like me. It is a cut-throat business and she wasn't strong enough to endure the harshness that it presented as most people in that field can be cruel and overly competitive. One day Steve and I received a call to please come and pick her up at work. She was so distressed about some things that had transpired at work that we had to call a psychiatrist immediately and take her in for a consultation. That was the end of a possible second career.

She finally decided to study Culinary Arts. That turned out to be her forte all along; she flourished and loves every minute of the food industry. She is a very talented Chef and her professors invited her to join them in Germany for the Culinary Arts Olympics.

She was asked and created a training video for New Mexico State University on the safety of poultry food handling. Most recently she taught a cooking class for semi-independent young adults with Down's syndrome.

Carrie and her husband Steve have three super neat boys and are currently expecting their fourth son. All five of them are such a blessing to both Steve and me. Like her brother, Carrie and her husband Steve home school their boys.[1]

---

1 Carrie has now given birth to their fourth son, another blessing and miracle.

CHAPTER TWENTY
Therapy 1982

A friend had casually mentioned the inner healing seminar being sponsored by Sophia Fellowship that would take place in a couple of weeks in Simi Valley, California. Where in the world was Simi Valley? I got lost easily and this was way out of my comfort zone; somehow I knew that I had to be there; that that's where my deeper healing would begin. Hemorrhagic nosebleeds were continuing, I was begging and praying for help.

My hand trembled as I picked up the phone, I dialed and waited. As the phone rang my hands became clammy and many thoughts went through my mind; maybe there is no one there to tend to the phones, maybe it's too late, etc., etc. It seemed like forever before someone answered, "Hello, St. Elizabeth's, can I help you"? The voice at the other end seemed friendly enough. "Uh, hello my name is Angela. I heard that you are hosting a seminar, one on inner healing". "Yes" came the reply, "we have it scheduled for May 16th through May 18th• starting at 6 pm. would you like to sign up?" "I first need to know if there is housing available and please tell me where Simi Valley is."

"I'm sorry but there is no more housing available. Are you familiar with the San Fernando Valley?" "No, but first let me think about what to do and where I'll stay". So many decisions for me to make (at 34 years of age I'd never been allowed to have any choices let alone make a decision). I'm a bit nervous, I replied. The kind voice said "please give us your number and if housing does become available we'll call you." As I hung up the phone, questions bombarded my mind. How would I get there, where would I stay, what about John and the kids? This was way too much for me to comprehend. Then I remembered what I learned and trusted that if God wants me there, I'll be there.

Scarcely five minutes had passed when the phone rang. "Hello this is Marie from St. Elisabeth's Parish. May I speak with Angela?" "Yes, I replied". "Great news, we have a couple here George & Irene that overheard your call earlier and they would love to share their home with you. What do you think?" I'm astonished; they don't even know me but yes of course, thank you. They must be some kind of Angels. Thank you Lord, I know that you hear my silent prayers and praise.

As the days followed I wondered with nervous anticipation what my new escapade would be like. May 16th. finally arrived; I reviewed my schedule again as I didn't want to arrive late or too early to inconvenience my hosts. They had also invited me to supper with them. Oh what a joy!

I remember the drive clearly; I drove and drove. There were lots of new things for me to see. It was both exciting and frightening as I passed industrial complexes, residential areas, patches of barren land, pastures and lovely, lush green hillsides.

I arrived at the home of Mr. and Mrs. George Oliver right on schedule. To my surprise there stood this elderly couple in their 80's but they had the energy and all the characteristics of someone in their 30's. A lovely gentle smile touched their lips, as though they knew me.

George and Irene embraced me in a loving way such as I'd never experienced. After all these years I truly believe that they were angels. God knows our needs and he never disappoints us.

When we arrived at the church where the seminar was to take place we received a warm and tender greeting. It was as though everyone knew George & Irene, but how? I answered myself "they're Angels".

The evening began with the introduction of all the speakers. I immediately focused on Terri & Timothy. I wondered if I would ever be whole as they were. I even fantasied about Timothy. Could a real man ever fall in love with me? I knew that I could prove to be a loving and nurturing partner. And Terri, she seemed so together, a real woman. I envisioned my wholeness as reality.

As the weekend progressed I began to wonder if I would be strong enough to undergo the intense therapy and process of growth. There is no halfway with me, it is or it isn't. There were times that I already felt segregated from other people. I knew that if I committed myself to the process of inner healing that I would be alone on this journey. My sisters were never supportive so I knew that I would spend the most painful of times alone. In fact, when I first went into any therapy their comments were not kind. "You must really be crazy," or "maybe, you're a split personality". I knew that pursuing wholeness would never be on their radar.

By Sunday I knew what I had to do. When the altar call came, I could hardly stay in my seat. My intense sobbing from previous similar situations crossed my mind but composed myself and thought that I could be cool about the whole thing if I went up.

I don't recall others rising as I approached Terri and said, "I need prayer, I'm going through a very painful time right now, can you help me? I'm recovering from childhood trauma and I am currently separated from my husband, but he recently moved back in. We live like brother and sister. I'm confused and get nosebleeds all the time, heavy ones like when I was a child."

At this point I'm sobbing uncontrollably and the nosebleed start with a heavy gush. We grabbed whatever was available or what was handed to us to control the onslaught of blood. I was escorted to a smaller room in back and the team followed and proceeded to lay hands on me and pray. They prayed for what seemed like forever. When the bleeding stopped I gained my composure and with their help cleaned up. I explained that I would seek counseling with them, thanked them and left. I thought, oh "God, will I ever stop crying and will the nosebleeds ever stop?"

So my commitment was made, I couldn't go on like this. In the months that followed I made numerous attempts to make an appointment to meet with Terri at Sophia Fellowship. I left repeated messages on their answering machine and still I didn't hear from them. No matter how urgent a message I left it went unheeded. This would be one of many obstacles that I was to encounter as I sought healing. I prayed for any interference to be removed and finally got a breakthrough.

All the while that I was trying to connect with Terri I'd been in psycho-therapy with a secular counselor but something was definitely lacking. My spirituality and relationship with Christ has always been at the forefront of my life and this was missing in my current therapy. How could someone help me if they didn't share the same views and understand that I'd survived without crutches because I loved Jesus so much and knew that he also loved and cared for me?

It took almost seven months to finally connect with Sophia Fellowship on January 8, 1983. A friend and I prayed incessantly about making a connection and it finally happened one day when Terri answered the phone. I explained that I'd been leaving messages since our first meeting. She said that her office hadn't received a single one. My first appointment was officially scheduled for January 27, 1983.

I was nervous about the appointment so I asked a friend to join me. I allowed myself two hours for what should have taken about forty-five minutes since I wasn't familiar with the area. I had not anticipated the number of obstacles that would interfere with my journey.

On the road to picking up my friend I narrowly missed being hit head on. I explained to her what had happened so we prayed before continuing on our journey. We hadn't driven ten minutes from her home when we had a tire blow-out on the freeway; I exited and pulled to a stop. Thank God that no cars were close by to obstruct our exit. It took only a few minutes for a courteous driver to come along and offer assistance to change our tire. The more obstacles we encountered, the more we prayed and the more determined I was to reach our destination.

My focus was the belief that God must have a miraculous plan for my life because by the time we were back on the road we'd lost over an hour. I knew that I wouldn't make my appointment on time but I'd proceed and let them know that I intended to be there. When we arrived, they said that my appointment had been filled and only after I explained the circumstance of my failure did they fully understand that intercessory prayer was indeed needed, so we prayed together and scheduled a new appointment.

My new appointment arrived without a hitch. As weeks of therapy turned into months my concern about survival was ever present. Thirty-four years of oppressed emotions started to take their toll and at times the pain seemed insurmountable. Terri suggested dream therapy as we believed that it might expedite the long tedious process of my healing. In all my sessions with her she'd lay hands on me and pray in tongues and I know that her prayers got me through many crises.

As therapy progressed she advised me to get involved in more physical activity and that the road to wholeness incorporates the mind, body and soul (emotional, physical and spiritual). I couldn't get into the physical exercise, as the energy I spent in inner healing was overwhelming. I left some sessions with an intense headache and sense of exhaustion. For periods of weeks and months I just existed. Faith was the driving force that kept me going. I had no emotional, spiritual or physical reserve left. I did what I could to protect the children from the battles that raged inside of me. I'd wait until they went away every other weekend visiting with their dad so that I could break down and I would spend the entire weekend sobbing and screaming. I asked Terri repeatedly "will all this stuff that I'm doing help my children"? The answer was always yes.

I acknowledged anger and hurt feelings which were primarily directed toward God. It concerned me that I could be angry at our Creator but I was reassured that it was OK to have those negative feelings. I knew that healing was occurring. At first infinitesimal, nevertheless I saw glimpses of it. Initially it came in the form of intense joy; joy such as I'd never experienced before. The nosebleeds eventually stopped, also the recurring laryngitis, and other common ailments like colds and sinus infections.

I begin to feel this deepening love for my children and others in my life. I always loved my kids but it was like the kind of love that Christ has for us. This was different; it was intense, compassionate and unconditional. It wasn't of me because I don't believe humans have the capacity to love this fully. I was awakening to The Holy Spirit love in my life.

My love for unborn, aborted babies still grips me to the core. I'm not completely sure yet but I have an intense connection to aborted babies. God will reveal that to me when he knows I am ready. I have an equally strong desire to rescue children and adults that are enslaved in any way.

Once when I was alone and was walking down our

long hallway at home I screamed at the top of my lungs "oh God, if you knew that this was going to happen why did you let us bring children into the world"? It was to be the first time that I audibly heard God speak to me; he actually yelled back "if I waited until my people were healthy there would be no children"! I was flabbergasted that Our Lord spoke to me and he seemed angry but I understood his reasoning.

On my first visit to Sophia Fellowship I started by explaining to Terri about a recurring dream and or vision.

I am being called by a voice in the Heavens. I wake up and eagerly respond, "I'm coming." This has occurred repeatedly for many, many years. It happened so frequently that my body would respond before even hearing the voice.

I see myself leaving my bed and lifting my head to an invisible being but with a voice that is gentle, kind and one which I trust completely. Whether it is a dream or vision there is always accuracy in the bedroom and location of where I'm currently living. I always heed the call willingly and eagerly though I don't know where I've gone once I've left my bed.

My antique bed was elaborate with decorative wood side rails. The first time that I was called after Carrie was born my body started responding as usual but this time was different. As I begin to drift up I grab onto the bed side rails, my legs are gently rising and I say "I can't come anymore, I have a daughter now and she needs me". I don't know what changed because I had continued to journey even after my sons were born.

Starting on July 6, 1985 through August 9, 1985,

I was having bad anxiety or panic attacks. I had never experienced them before but maybe it's because I'd blocked so much from my mind so that I could function in a semblance of normalcy.

August 12, 1986 was the first time that I started writing my book; my dreams begin to change profoundly. I'd been in a dry season as far as dreams. This was the beginning of many dubious dreams.

"I awakened very early in the morning. It seems that my bedroom is parallel to that of my mother's with both rooms having a sliding exterior door at the end of the room facing the foot of the bed. There is no physical wall to separate the two rooms. I'm aware of my mother in her bed, sound asleep and the presence of another person in my bed also asleep. I don't know who that person is, though I sit up in bed and look outdoors. In the sky I see what appears to be a small round army-green flying saucer. Something is falling from it like ashes on fire.

I get out of bed and go outdoors for a closer look. To my surprise there are many, and all of them are dropping the same sort of burning ashes. Now they seem to be directed at our sliding doors. I rush inside and proceed to close the glass door quickly as it has been open except for the closed screen door.

A burning chunk of ash comes in and a few sparks fly off. I finish closing the glass door. My mother's door has been closed from the beginning. I get into bed with mother. I hug and kiss her. I tell her how much I love her and I realize how lonely she must be not having a man to share her life with. I wake up and am repulsed by the dream.

I planned to discuss this with Terri as up until now I have no awareness of the abuse that I'd endured at the hands of my mother.

> Your remembrances are like unto ashes…. Job 13:12
> Is not My word like as a fire? Saith the Lord; and like a hammer that breaketh the rock (stony heart) in pieces? Jeremiah 23:29 KJV

As healing progressed I could no longer remain married. I had known for a long time that we wouldn't succeed unless we both put effort into it. We had a couple of counseling sessions together but accomplished nothing. My husband was not ready to bare his soul and shortly thereafter we separated and started divorce proceedings.

I'm going through a divorce from my first husband, maybe it's not too late to save my son Armando's shattered spirit caused by his abusive father. I reach out to my mother-I pray that time has softened her heart and replaced her bitterness with compassion. Her words pierce my heart more than if she had driven a sword directly into it. "Pendeja, stay with him, you can't do any better, nobody wants you, Fea (ugly)".

While many changes were taking place in my life I couldn't forgive myself for breaking up my marriage. The guilt I felt was overwhelming and the enemy used it to criticize and castigate me every opportunity that I allowed. Recovering from the guilt I felt wouldn't come for several years.

CHAPTER TWENTY-ONE
Major Roadblock

In 1986 while in therapy I hit a major road block. It had been weeks since I made any progress and knew that it would be too painful to allow whatever was standing in the way to surface. I added to my weekly therapy sessions, inner healing seminars, prayer groups, and still nothing. My pain was so great that I thought if I allowed it to surface that it would actually suffocate me. It felt like a growth that began forming in my lungs and went clear up to the base of my throat and at times I felt like I couldn't breathe.

It was at this time that I stopped seeing Terri. She said that she couldn't keep taking my money and that when God felt I was ready he would open that wound. I heard about a powerful prayer group that met in another city. It was about an hour's drive from where I lived. They met you on an individual basis and prayed until they received spiritual direction. I met with them weekly without making any progress. Eventually they referred me to a Charismatic Priest who conducts inner healing services. Father Jim laid hands on me and spoke of deep oppression but again no progress or deliverance was made; he suggested daily communion if possible. I thought how much more spiritual can I become. My pursuit for healing ended here and I needed some down time.

The burden of healing, raising three children, working, maintaining a household was grueling and it was taking its toll on my body and my spirit. I had lost so much weight that I had to shop in the pre-teen department of most stores; I wore size 0-1. During this journey I didn't even take much time to eat. I worked across the street from a Winchell's Donut shop so my mainstay was a quick cup of coffee and a donut; I learned that you can lose weight by just eating donuts if you eat nothing else.

During this same period I got really sick and not surprisingly had become hypoglycemic.

I understand why so many people in need don't pursue the healing process. It's painful and at times the progress is miniscule. That doesn't even take into consideration the financial cost of achieving wholeness. There is help available if you're an alcoholic or drug user but there is no help if you want to achieve healing and wholeness through Christ.

I believe that this is where churches have failed. They have not considered and made provision for healing the wounds, lies and curses that we enter into this world with or that are projected onto us by broken parents.

I had spent so many years in therapy. Much later I learned about Sozo Ministry. It is a Greek word meaning "made whole, healed and delivered". I believe that a few Sozo Ministry sessions would have expedited my healing. I know that it was the catalyst that brought me to the next phase of my life.

Recovery is a journey, a difficult one at that and it

takes commitment and sacrifice. I repeatedly asked my therapist about the end game as it was so painful. If it would help my children I could do it, I didn't have enough self-worth to carry the pain, if it was just for me. The picture was much larger than I.

CHAPTER TWENTY-TWO
1989 Thrown to the Wolf

Growing up, our birthdays were not acknowledged so my sisters and I always made an effort to have parties and festivities to celebrate the life of our children. On this particular day we looked forward to another joyous celebration. The children always had a blast getting together. Each of us had two boys and one girl, the boy's favorite pastime was wrestling, laughing and carrying on. The dad's would barbecue and play cards. We all loved the get-togethers and the parties.

We arrived at my sister's house to celebrate my nephew's birthday.[2] I watched in horror as my mother came up to my daughter, patted her on the face in what should have been a very loving gesture, then came her words "mira, fea, equal a su mama"! My little girl asked me what grandma said? I told her that it was nothing important. I couldn't tell her that her piercing words were "look, she's ugly just like her Mother!" I know now that mom was assaulting me for all that she'd done to me that made her feel ugly. Her goal was to continue hurting me by attacking my precious daughter. This was the only

---

2   As were getting ready to go to print the Holy spirit gave me the following insight. Mother saw a window of opportunity to attack me and my lovely daughter because she glimpsed the purity and love that Carrie and I have for one another; something that she and I never had. There was envy in her words.

way that she could continue to strike me with her venom.

I told the girls that I was leaving because I couldn't stand it anymore. Their comments were that mom was only kidding because that was mother's "go to phrase" whenever she said something mean and vicious and tried to clean up her poisonous words. "What is wrong with you girls......this is unbelievable and unforgiveable!"

My anger surfaced even as I tried to suppress deep repressed painful emotions. My reply came smooth and calculated. "I've spent my whole life trying to overcome all the damage and harm that you did to me. I won't tolerate your rudeness or meanness anymore".

My sisters were still afraid to call her on her ongoing bad behavior. They were little girls petrified to have a voice or an opinion. They just wouldn't attest to the fact that we were ever abused.

This reminded me of a story that Bonnie shared about grandmother when my youngest son asked her what she was like. Her response was hilarious and really sad at the same time. "When Beth and I were little we were at grandmas and did something that she didn't approve of. She tied a rope around our waist and hung us up from the porch rafters to show passing cars that we were bad. We must have done something to deserve it"! WOW! I've yelled at them and said "wake up". It's almost too painful to be around them.

However, once again I felt betrayed as I was thrown to the wolf. I was ready to put her in her place and just leave. My sister's took me into the bedroom and begged me not to "rock the boat", that it would hurt mother's feelings and they didn't want to see her cry (crying was another form of mothers manipulation) as they were still so afraid of her. I replied "what about us"? Because of their fear of her they would go on protecting her even to this day even though she passed away many years ago. My sister's argument is that mom did the best she could. Oh really! That evening I fought to contain the explosive emotions that battered one another. I'd wait until I was alone the following day. I knew that the explosion waiting to erupt within me would frighten the children and I wondered whether or not to call Terri. The battle raging inside could no longer be contained. Could I handle it? I had skills that I'd learned in many years of therapy and decided to face this one alone. As evening turned into night I felt the volcano prepare to do its destruction. Thoughts came quickly, one painful memory after another.

As soon as the kids got off to school I quickly closed the blinds and turned off the answering machine. The monster within was already gnawing its way to the surface. The sobbing came like a violent storm engulfing me in rage, fear, pain and even hatred. Once again I was suffocating; there was a lead brick right in the middle of my chest. I tried pushing it off. I couldn't get enough air. God help me I cried, I'm losing it, help me!

Hours later I pieced myself together in anticipation of the children returning from school. I had bouts of crying throughout the week but little by little I began to feel better. I couldn't wait to get back to therapy and share with Terri. I made peace with myself and with mother, I grieved for her and my sisters circumstances as I knew that they would never in this life find the true harmony, peace or joy that comes from healing.

Over the next few years I had very little to do with mother. I had to extricate myself from her and from my sisters. I was furious at them as well and it was time to break off this toxic relationship as I needed time and space to heal.

My Dark Night of the Soul

I experienced what fifteen century Christian writer St. John of the Cross referred to as la noche escura (Dark Night of the Soul). My dark night was spiritual and psychological.

My external circumstances were emotionally crippling and overwhelming that my only viable course of action was to completely surrender and find rest in Jesus. In the process I received extraordinary grace and spiritual awakening. I was at a place where God had to purge me thoroughly of my old self that was utterly broken so that I could experience a new and deeper love for Jesus, others and myself. In this process I found greater intimacy with the Holy Spirit.

Did I trust God to see me through it? My emotions were raw as I screamed out, help me, I'm drowning. God had to completely strip me of any doubt that I may have had regarding my faith and know with certainty that he was omnipotent, omniscient and omnipresent in my life.

Sometimes the external circumstances during the Dark Night can get so uncomfortable and overwhelming that it traps you into a spot where the only way to get out is to love, trust, accept and surrender; because our ego can be addicted to suffering. Trust in this process and know that you will not be incapacitated and you will rise victorious.

This too shall pass. Jesus invites us in our weariness to find rest in him.

> Matthew 11:28 NIV "Come to me, all you who are weary and burdened, and I will give you rest.
>
> Psalm 112:4 NIV Even in darkness light dawns for the upright, for those who are gracious and compassionate and righteous.
>
> John 1:5 NIV the light shines in the darkness and the darkness has not overcome

Because of all the years that I lived in darkness; when I am lied to or manipulated, anger still rises in me. I'm on a journey where there seems to be no end in sight but I will not be discouraged.

CHAPTER TWENTY-THREE
"Throw the Pan"

John 9:6-7 After saying this, he spit on the ground, made some mud with the saliva, and put it on the man's eyes. "Go," he told him, "wash in the Pool of Siloam" (this word means "Sent"). So the man went and washed, and came home seeing. NIV

Sometimes the Lord will tell us to do something that sounds outrageous and we don't understand, but if your heart is open to his prompting he won't let you down.

My daughter and sons had returned from a weekend visit with their dad. It was late in the evening so we only had little time to visit as it was already close to bedtime. They took their baths, said their prayers and went to bed.

Monday morning arrived almost too soon. I was still tired but I put myself in a good mood looking forward to starting the week on a positive note. I didn't want to think about all the previous mornings after they'd spent a weekend with their dad. Their emotional needs weren't met, and I always faced the brunt of their frustration. The boys were best friends but always returned home moody, sad and cranky.

Since I drove them all to Whittier Christian School

in a neighboring town I usually prepared a breakfast that they could enjoy during the thirty minute ride. Today I was preparing my version of a famous fast food breakfast sandwich. My large heavy skillet sizzled with four over-medium eggs layered on thick ham slices and melted cheese. The English muffins were about to pop out of the toaster.

As is normal after a visit with their dad, the boys start bickering. "Lord, I can't go through this again," as their arguing escalates. "God, please make them stop you know my nerves are already frayed." My calm demeanor starts to erode. I try really hard to keep peace and a semblance of normalcy and not let the whole situation of the divorce and healing cause any more uncertainty or fear come into their lives. I work two jobs but the finances are always tight with school, therapy and overall living expenses; but I still manage to maintain tranquility.

Since my income was greater than my husbands, child support was miniscule at only $300.00 per month. If that wasn't enough my attorney had to fight in court so that I wouldn't have to pay the alimony to my ex-husband that his attorney was requesting.

Just as I'm about to break down and collapse on the floor I'm telling the Lord "I can't take this anymore". What the Lord responds with next; shocks me back into reality. He says "throw the pan." "What!" I don't think I heard him correctly. I'm thinking I'm on a tight budget and can't waste food. The boys are arguing, my daughter is now on edge but once again now louder and very clear I hear "throw the pan as hard as you can!"

I don't want to throw anything and frighten my

children. That's what my mother used to do (for different reasons, but still). I don't want to do that and I'm really conflicted as there are so many thoughts going through my mind. I'm thinking about the cost of the food as I glance across the room, oh wow those are glass French doors and it will cost a lot to fix them. This time the voice is louder "throw it - get their attention". I can't believe that I'm doing what I'm doing but now I'm absolutely certain that it's the Lord's voice. In an instant I grab the handle of a very heavy 14" diameter, quarter inch thick skillet as though it weights nothing and with as much force as I can muster I fling it across the kitchen passing right through the family room. I aim straight at the glass, about 30 feet away, the eggs fly off and with the yoke become glued to the ceiling. The skillet bounces off the French doors. To my shock and delight nothing breaks. The side of the skillet that hit bends as though it's made of tin but not a single break in the glass. Thank you Lord! I got scared, the boys and my daughter got scared but I got their attention. "This bickering will not happen every time you come home". That was the end of that.

On a side note-I left the eggs on the ceiling for the remaining years that we lived in that house as a reminder to the boys about what the Lord said to do. And for those of you that know me, know what an eyesore those eggs were, my home was spotless except for some yolks and egg white dangling off of the ceiling. It was disgusting and funny at the same time and there were never any flies attracted to my "masterpiece". Oh, what joy.

CHAPTER TWENTY-FOUR
Successes

By 1989 I'd been in counseling continuously for almost ten years. I'd been single for about eight years and had maintained healthy platonic and romantic relationships. I'd had successful jobs. I even made a temporary career change and took a job at a college so that one of my sons could get his tuition paid. By now I had had many successes. My miniature Lighted Christmas made it on the cover of Miniature Collector Magazine. Life was good but I still had work to do as I continued on my journey to wholeness.

    I had dated and had many marriage proposals even one from a Saudi Prince. If I wouldn't marry him would I at least consider being his personal assistant? He had many business entities in the United States and he explained that while taking care of business he was often taken advantage of. He said that I had the most integrity of anyone he'd met in the states and he trusted me completely. It would have been an exciting venture but at the time I still had children at home and I wouldn't accept his offer of a new career or of a live-in nanny.

    One evening he called and said that we were going to a party in Florida in his private jet. I couldn't go as I had the children that weekend. He said that he could bring a nanny to stay with them but I declined. No way was I going to leave my kids with a stranger.

Whenever he was in California we'd meet for dinner on a casual basis. I had my own business at the time and received calls from him frequently. I'd introduce him to girlfriends that he could date but nothing ever came of the meetings.

We got along good because we had a mutual respect for one another. Sadly my relationship ended with Aziz not long after my invitation to the party in Florida. He was in town and was hosting a party at a large hotel for some big wigs and he wanted me to come and bring a couple of single girlfriends. I went but only invited one friend whom he had previously met. About the same time an unnamed famous actor walked in, Aziz's bodyguard returned from running an errand. He returned with a bag of cocaine and as soon as I learned what they were doing I left alone. My girlfriend wanted to stay so that was about the last I saw of her as well.

I always had healthy platonic relationships with males because of the message that we got growing up that men weren't any good and couldn't be trusted, so I made it a point to prove that advice as incorrect.

I also had a few proposals from some of my buddies though I wasn't at the point of getting married again anytime soon and besides we just goofed around like brother and sister. I desired wholeness first before getting involved with anyone. When I'd travel for business with married male friends their spouses always wanted them to hang out with me because they knew that with me they were safe from the advances of other females and that I could be trusted. At least one of my friends was a single dad so we did things together with the kids.

CHAPTER TWENTY-FIVE
He's An Oak

My best girlfriend since high school had worked with Steve for several years. They acted like siblings and had a professional working relationship. On a couple of occasions she would tell me about him and say that he wanted to meet me. I wasn't interested as I had already been dating a really great guy for a few years. My kids liked him and together with his daughter we'd do many fun things together.

As I grew emotionally I made decisions that were in my best interest. I decided to close this chapter in my life and move on. I told Evelyn that I would meet her friend Steve, since I always had "buddy friends" and it wouldn't hurt to have another. She introduced us and we've been together ever since. Steve is brilliant, handsome, and I loved the way he respected his parents and was always concerned for their well-being.

We got married in a lovely little chapel at Knott's Berry Farm in southern California. We have grown together and spiritually we are on the same page. He's a great step-dad to our grown kids and a great grandpa. I think that his super power is being a grandpa.

I shared earlier about Christiaan and how he is forever into busyness or mischief. We are at the chapel ready to get married; the pianoist, the singer, and the entire bridal party are present, with one exception. Where's Christaan? We are about to start the ceremony without him when he shows up, soaked from head to toe. He has been riding the "log ride" in his tuxedo. And that my friends sums up the true Christiaan.

By society standards our lives are pretty boring, for us it is exactly as it should be. We read together, play games, watch movies and love to play Legos with our grandkids. He's an engineer so spends his extra time building mechanical things in the garage. He's an EMT, a volunteer fire fighter and a Certified Water Systems Operator. I spend my time creating things in my designing/sewing room. We attend bible study and take personal growth classes when they are available. Steve is my oak.

CHAPTER TWENTY-SIX
Stirring

I became obsessed with writing. I wrote down every dream and each successive one intensified about relationships, violence and discovery. I was forced to study and evaluate past and present acquaintances. What was the purpose of each in my life and mine in theirs?

After careful examination I separated myself from some and concentrated on those friendships that I felt I could trust. I'd stopped being concerned about my worth to them rather their value to me. In the past I'd discounted me and mine and had lived like no more than a parasite or fungus. As I healed I learned to appreciate my needs first rather than those of others.

The years that I'd spent being an extension of what I was molded to be were over. All the while I was suffocating and dying a slow death. The scripture about setting the captives free always came to mind. I'd been imprisoned for so long. Never again, I had finally tasted freedom.

I was fifty-eight years old when the wall of blocked memories collapsed. I wake up from a sound sleep in June, 2005 with this sick and disgusting feeling, tears start rolling down the side of my face onto my pillow.

The words out of my mouth were like vinegar on an

open wound. "Mom, I can't do this anymore, I don't have to do this anymore, I won't do this anymore. I have another bedroom, Steve built us a big house, I can sleep on my own bed". As I lay on my side with a heavy arm wrapped around my waist my first body memories start to emerge. As I push it away I realize that it is my husband's arm, not my mother's. I jump out of bed as memories start to envelope me and I begin to shake violently. Oh God, oh God why? This pain and shame can only come from the pit of hell.

Between sobs, questions start to engulf me into conscious knowing and being fully aware of the abyss that I've just emerged from. How can this be I ask myself, yet not shocked or surprised; my knowing comes into full awareness. Burning rage rises from deep inside and a pain that causes me to double over as I attempt to get out of bed. What kind of monster does this to her child? Men molest; mothers don't! At least that's what I thought up until now. Mothers are supposed to nurture, comfort and teach children.

This was disgusting and degrading as images manifested themselves I begin to feel an unspeakable anger toward mother and my sisters. It's too much, how does something like this happen in a civilized world. Why didn't they protect me? I was the youngest and they didn't look out for me. How did they not know what was going on. They chose to look the other way. Didn't they question that my nose hemorrhages always occurred in mother's presence. My spirit was using the only defense that I had. If I'm bleeding she can't touch me. The fear I had of her would have caused anyone to question that something was wrong.

One sister callously would ask "why do you always have this pained look on your face-like there is a deep sadness. She would even confer with my cousin Jimmy about my lack of joy, that I never looked happy. There was never any benevolence in her questions only critical assessment. Really! Being raped on a regular basis doesn't make for a happy face!

I understand why I remembered very little from age three when my daddy left until nine or ten. I also had intermittent periods of memory loss until I was about fourteen or fifteen.

Did my therapist Terri know all along but couldn't tell me. I know that she respected her code of ethics and couldn't put any thoughts in my head. Revelation can only come from the patient. The only thing she could say to me was that we're at a roadblock and that the Lord will bring that wall down when he knows that I am ready.

My sisters and I were all in survival mode. They don't claim that we were abused but they are naive. We were all victims in one way or another. There was nothing that we could do to please our mother as she was always angry.

The holidays were the most difficult for all of us. Mother always seemed to get intoxicated near Thanksgiving and Christmas. It wasn't unusual for her to crash her car this time of year but the accidents were never her fault; maybe a post just got in her way.

No answer that the girls offer for not guarding me will ever be satisfactory. In their defense I emphatically believe that they were just enduring the days and were crippled by their own fear. They didn't want to rock the boat or cause any more chaos lest they become targets. They have apologized but that will never reverse the exploitation that they allowed me to endure. It has taken my entire life to overcome the cruelty I received at the hands of our mother.

They claim absolute ignorance that, while I was away in a tryst being lasciviously abused, they had no reason to question. One sister reminds me that I must have been a favorite or why else would mom insist that I spend long periods of time alone with her. That I was called ugly and Raton (Rat) didn't ring any bells that there was some sort of contradiction there. I wasn't ugly, mother was projecting, she felt ugly inside because of what she was doing to me.

I wonder which of them was also violated in the same manner. Bonnie manifests behavior of someone who has been sexually abused. Although she is not consciously aware of it she suffers from multiple health and emotional issues, always claiming victimhood. When she was little she'd have these terrifying dreams and gut wrenching screams. She claimed to see the devil himself.

I recall a smell that I can't seem to shake. It was always present while alone with mother. Like a hormonal smell, not offensive or repulsive just a weird smell. I think I remember her taking some kind of injections but that is also fuzzy in my mind. I've asked my sisters about both things but they have no knowledge or recall of anything related. I believe that it was during these rituals that the abuse occurred. I still don't understand how or why but I know that there is a connection.

Mother called me a whore and maybe she called my

sisters that as well. We weren't whores but she was projecting what and how she may have felt about herself. That is one reason I believe that I wasn't the only one that was abused. I know I didn't have pre-marital sex and to my knowledge neither did my sisters. I remember feeling dirty after I started my periods. I had become unclean and untouchable but maybe that is what saved me from continued abuse as I entered my teens.

I'm embarrassed and ashamed that my husband also knows the secret that has been buried about my past. How could I even begin to express to him how mortified I am that I was nothing more than a sex object. Abused by the one person that is supposed to love and protect you. Lifetimes have passed since the revelation of all that I endured but the sting is always present. It would take years for me to begin to comprehend; I was so angry and at times still furious that my sisters didn't do anything to intervene.

After mother passed away in 2006 the images of the invisible attacker ceased. I could never fight her off but she can no longer hurt me. Her sexual sin of the flesh overpowered her.

Once again as previously in my life I'd wait until I was alone to have fits of crying, sobbing and yelling at God. I felt so raw, broken and dirty. How does this happen? I will never fully understand except that I know factually and have firsthand knowledge that there is evil in the world.

It's extremely important to acknowledge the sexual immorality that happened to my son comes from the same bloodline curse that caused my mother to sexually abuse me. Let's call it what it is; incest perpetrated by a family member on the same gender is nothing less than homosexuality.

I had started to understand why I was punished, because as I was getting older I was able to hold back my body and take control of it, although I have no distinct memory of doing so.

Good memories are wonderful but bad memories buried deep can also be good if you're on a path to emotional wholeness. They make themselves known when you are ready. They can be used to heal and serve you.

CHAPTER TWENTY-SEVEN
Cancer & Redemption

I don't know if it's ironic or a coincidence that the same month and year that I had my first body memory is the same year that mother got really sick and was diagnosed with inoperable stomach cancer.

In the summer of 2005 mother started to get really bad stomach pain. By late fall she was at home on hospice care. The stomach cancer had spread rapidly. A tumor had wrapped itself around her intestines. There was nothing that could be done for her.

We were all by her side and let her know that it was alright to let go as she was in acute pain and struggling to stay alive. She did not want to die. By now she was in a semi-conscious state where the lucid mind takes over. Holding up her right hand she said something strange and mysterious, "there are five".

Mother passed away in January, 2006. We wouldn't go on to figure out the puzzle she'd left us with until July 2007 when Belle came into our lives.

Another weird thing she said was "I want to take all you girls with me". We looked at each and said "oh no, you can't take us, we aren't ready". How's that for a shocker and why would she even think of that. I recently repented on her behalf, so that curse for an early death doesn't land on any of us.

Two days before she passed I was alone with her and with tears rolling down her cheeks she said "I'm sorry". She couldn't speak very much but I knew what she meant. My own tears are streaming down my face and I reply "I know and I forgive you". I'd waited my whole life to hear kind words from my mother.

I made peace with myself and with her. I grieved for her and her circumstances. I pray that she's in a better place where she can find tranquility. I've forgiven her but have no desire to visit her gravesite.

CHAPTER TWENTY-EIGHT
Unexplainable Yearning

I often spoke of and felt a deep yearning, a loss, brokenness, as though a part of me was missing. I couldn't put my finger on what it was and I never understood it until we received a phone call in 2007.

I was at work and I get a phone call from my sister Bonnie. I was very busy and offered to call back; she was insistent that it could not wait. In a matter of seconds she practically screams the words that still echo in my ears "we have another sister"!

As the tears start rolling down my cheeks, I respond with "I know". I'd known most of my life without knowing that I knew. God gives us a gift of intuition through our limbic system that even when our conscious doesn't know you can bet that the unconscious mind does. You can call it instinct, sixth sense, hunch or whatever but you know that you know. I knew that a part of me was out there someplace. In the days that followed I felt a sense of peace and wholeness.

Two weeks later my husband, daughter and I drove to Albuquerque to meet Belle. As we sit across a table staring at each other in disbelief my husband says that it's like watching twins meet for the first time, yes, Belle and I are that much alike.

Belle had known most of her life that she was adopted. As an adult she had hired an adoption search service to find her natural mother but it would be years before she would find us.

It wasn't until one year and seven months after mother passed away that Belle located us. The timing was perfect according to God's law. I believe that had her search found us while mother was alive we wouldn't have the privilege of knowing her today as mom was very proud and maintaining her image was paramount. She would never have admitted to having a child out of wedlock. I believe Belle is the secret mother thought she took with her to the grave, because when she held up her hand, and said "there are five" we had no idea what she was talking about.

Another peculiarity is that the adoption papers clearly stated that Belle had four siblings, three sisters and one brother. This further supported my belief that I really was a disappointment.

Belle's parents tell the story that they couldn't conceive a child and proceeded to adopt. In anticipation of having their "own" child they would go to the doctor at the same time that the birth mother would go for her regular visits to keep track of the progress. They were attentive and grateful that they would soon have a child. Once, as they waited for the outcome of my mother's visit they were able to glance into the examining room. They saw that mother wore a tight bandage across her abdomen to pull in her stomach. This is how she was able to conceal her pregnancy for a very long time.

Belle had a much different life than we had. She

was adopted by an affluent couple. Her family traveled extensively and even lived abroad at times. Her father was a famous music composer and director. He composed music for the likes of Frank Sinatra and created the musical arrangement for the inauguration of President John Kennedy.

My new sister wore custom made shoes to correct her flat feet. We wore hand me downs that never fit quite right, causing blisters and callouses at the back of our heels. The contrast in our lives was palatable yet she and I both yearned for more. We both knew and felt that something supernatural was missing in our lives.

Our baby sister Belle is brilliant, worldly and sophisticated. Both in looks and personality she resembles the actress Fran Drescher from the hit show the Nanny.

In Belle's own words "Reflections on when I first met you and my sisters!"

There is always a searching process going on inside any adoptee's mind throughout their life! I believe I waited to search for my birth family after my father (daddy's girl I was) passed away in 1999. Children desire and feel the need for connection in a family, as all families regardless on which continent they may reside, are always comparing the looks and mannerisms of babies to their parents. It's a human connection, its science, it just is! I spent my growing up years always feeling like the adopted child, as my mother was white skinned and I olive with other physical characteristics unlike my parents. I loved to be around my Puerto Rican Aunt Terry, as she although was not olive skinned she was brown eyed like me and hugged me so very close to her when we visited.

When I found the information about my birth family, that there were three sisters and not two sisters and a brother I was in shock, ecstatic and well, almost no words other than there are four souls out there who share the same DNA as I!

People ask me and what about your father, I say" Well I have an idea but no confirmation, and actually maybe will look into it next year, but because my sisters albeit half-sisters (unless Juan was my dad) treat me as if I were a full blooded sister".

When I spoke to each sister at the on start of this new life journey, it was a very different feeling with each one of them, since they are alike in some ways, but different as well. The first sister I actually spoke to was my sister Bonnie (2nd in line) and she was cautious and questioning like what did I look like! Of course this came as a shock to all.

When speaking to my sister Bibiana (3rd in line) she was very emotional and was overwhelmed and perplexed as to how no one knew. Then there is my little sister Angela, who immediately heard my voice and said "I always knew you were out there", and that made feel so very special in that moment. My last and oldest sister Beth was emotional as well, however, I felt an almost sadness and guilt in her voice, as to how could this have happened without her or Bonnie knowing, being the oldest.

There are so many feelings attached to a process

such as what we have all experienced since 2007. I will never forget when I made the call to Grandpa George inquiring about a family member of mine, Sophia, and how he broke down on the phone and called me Hijita, after explaining that I had been adopted as a baby. My birth certificate in the hospital first read: "Baby Carbajal". However, I will never know just how hard this process was for our mother, I do not fault her, but thank her. My only sadness is not having had a lifetime with my four amazing loving sisters.

Sis, I hope this is a help, I may have gone off the message but there is so much to say, but mostly it's gratefulness to God for having given me the chance to find the sisters of my life who were out there and in fact closer than I knew when we lived in California until 1960. Also, when we moved back in 1969, and lived in Ventura County.
Love and kisses.
Your little sis forever Belle

CHAPTER TWENTY-NINE
Mother Was Always Angry

We were always supposed to keep the house clean. Once mom came home from work early and the dishes weren't washed. She took every dish and threw them out the back door onto the concrete breaking every one of them. Now we were still poor but with no dishes!

We were all between four and twelve years old. Any outburst like this terrified us as we never knew what would come next from her rage.

My sister's memories are muddled when it comes to anything negative about mother but I have to live in reality. I spent too much time escaping truth. There was physical, verbal, emotional and, in my case, all the above plus the sexual abuse. I pleaded to be hit, to be physically hurt rather than be the recipient of her poisonous words as anything would have been better.

Maybe the guilt mother felt for giving up our sister for adoption is what drove her to drinking heavily especially around the holidays since Belle was born in the fall. But then she was never happy any other time of the year either. Mom could render any seemingly sane male into someone total unruly.

When I was seventeen I got a call from the hospital. Mom was in the emergency room. She had been brutally beaten by some man in a bar. I walked into the room and the stench of alcohol wavered in the air enveloping the entire room. It was stagnant and if there was a color it would have been a dark gloomy gray. I was embarrassed but felt no empathy. I wanted to run and hide.

Another sad but memorable event was when one of my uncles was living with us. He had been shot in his head during WWII. He suffered greatly from the steel plate that was put in his skull. He was lying in bed one evening and for reasons that I don't recall, mom verbally went off on him. He did what he could to restrain himself but she hammered and hammered him until he lost it. He would have killed her that night had it not been for my sisters that hid her and tricked him. They told him that she had fled out through the bedroom window; shortly after this incident he moved out never to be heard from again.

CHAPTER THIRTY
An Advocate

About the last fifteen years of mother's life, Bonnie had become the main target of her cruelty. Mother fought with her all the time and made her the recipient of nasty notes and phone calls. I thought why now; hadn't we been through enough? By now I had become pretty outspoken and one day I told mom that her cruelty was unacceptable, "I put up with it because as a child I had no choice". Today I have alternatives but Bonnie didn't have a voice, she still couldn't speak her mind and for speaking out I became an outcast and as it turned out mom shut me out for months. Not a problem! I had become an advocate for the underdog.

I'd done the same in college when an African American classmate of mine was getting reamed for a simple infraction. I knew that this particular student drove about three plus hours to get to class on time. On this particular morning, warning had been given that the storms were severe and that you should stay indoors unless it was absolutely necessary to drive as the streets were flooded everywhere. She had been on the road more than five hours but still arrived a few minutes late.

This particular instructor allowed zero tolerance for absence or tardiness and wanted to expel her. It was early in the semester so none of us had had time to form friendships but that didn't matter. I went into combat mode and ended taking the whole event to the department head and didn't let up until justice was served and she was allowed to remain in class.

To this day we don't understand why Bonnie was so bullied. We have our suspicions but nothing concrete. Even during the last two remaining weeks before the cancer took mother's life she was still fighting with her; accusing, yelling and cursing her. Sometimes an individual will get like this because of mental illness but this wasn't the case with mom as her mind was still sharp.

I told Bonnie that she didn't have to be there but she stayed until she herself was hospitalized for what we thought was a heart attack but it turned out to be a severe panic attack. Bonnie still has many ailments and I pray that she will also find peace and good health while still on this earth. Most likely she will never embark on a journey to wholeness because you have to thoroughly desire deliverance. Once you embark on recovery from severe abuse you're entering a battleground with the enemy that he will fight you for. Remember that God is a very big God and the enemy is small. You must keep your focus on Christ.

I would like to be helpful to anyone who has been abused in any way, also in stopping sex trafficking and abortion. In many ways my life resonates with these two exploits. My prayer is that our Lord will use me in that arena. For his purpose, not mine. I want to make a difference. I can't imagine that my recovery was only for me.

CHAPTER THIRTY-ONE
Closure

I was finally at a place where I needed closure and desperately wanted to find Terri my therapist. Over the prior ten years I'd looked for her with no luck. I knew that she'd retired and told myself that if God wants me to find her I would. I started making phone calls and then I remembered that twenty some years earlier she volunteered at a women's shelter in Los Angeles. I prayed and started calling catholic shelters. I'd introduce myself and say something like "I know that all information is confidential but that I'd like to leave a message for anyone that might know a volunteer by such and such a name. She was my therapist for many years and please give her my phone number if anyone there knows her". I made many calls but never believed that my investigative research to find her was futile. I knew that it was just a matter of time because God promises us the desires of our heart?

About two hours passed and the phone rang. Our conversation went something like this:

Terri-"Hello Angela, oh my goodness this is Terri".

Me-"I can hardly believe that it's really you"

Terri-"I'm calling a number with the same prefix as mine. I'm in Magdalena, where do you live?"

Me-I reply that I'm in New Mexico and I'm in total disbelief. "I'm only an hour or so away from you."

Unbeknown to me was that when she retired she had returned to her roots where she grew up. All the years that I spent with her I never knew that we both originated from New Mexico. We had met in California and by providence we both ended up in our home state. It's miraculous, but not surprising that our paths crossed; this is how Our Lord works. Terri no longer practiced nor was she licensed to counsel in New Mexico. She did agree to see me on a personal basis; we visited a couple of times and I was able to find closure and move on and close a huge chapter in my life.

It has been one heck of a ride, like on a roller coaster without a seatbelt. Yet, my greatest regret is that, had I not spent so much time recovering and gained self confidence in my teens I would have had what one considers "a career with greater accomplishments". I would have done so much more.

CHAPTER THIRTY-TWO
Role Model

Mother always encouraged cleanliness and she'd say "even if people are poor doesn't mean that they have to be dirty". Despite the turbulence we lived with there were several basic life skills that we were taught. Mother worked hard and we had to work hard and there was no rest on weekends either. My sisters and I all worked at an early age. Be honest, don't steal, work hard and don't lie. Our lives were like a play titled "Oxymoron". You see if we weren't perfect girls her image might get tarnished.

The house always had to be tidy and we wore clean clothes. Remember the broken dishes? Well that never happened again.

Mother was an excellent cook. Working at diverse restaurants she learned to cook various types of ethnic foods. All of my sisters, my own kids, nieces, and nephews are great cooks. Our daughter is a professional chef. Cooking and entertaining is in our genes. Even Belle who joined our family much later in life is an extraordinary cook. Maybe it was our family that made the Shew-bread for the Jewish Temple. Shew-bread was unleavened bread placed upon a table which stood in the sanctuary together with the seven-branched candlestick and the altar of incense.

After mother got on her feet with steady work she was really good at finances and always had money saved. Though she didn't have a formal education she was street savvy.

She bought beautiful tailored women's suits and had a remarkable eye for stylish clothes.

She paid cash for cars and bought a brand new home in a nice neighborhood.

I don't ever recall her buying us anything even when she was in a position to do so. When we worked our earnings still had to be turned over to her. I had to ask for money that I earned to buy fabric when I needed to make some new clothes. I don't know why but Bonnie was allowed to buy herself lots of clothes and beautiful furniture for her room. She would spend much of her income on clothes. When she got married she had new clothes in chests and closets that were never worn. She still shops a lot and it seems to give her a temporary sense of fulfillment and self-worth. The amount of clothes and furniture that Bonnie was allowed to buy was another contradiction in the way mother treated us.

Bibiana and I are total clean freaks and organization is paramount to our sense of wellbeing. These were things that she and I could control, but on the down side Bibiana has become more and more domineering of those around her. Fear causes her to be controlling just like mother was. I believe that as long as she has Beth to protect her actions and motives she'll never change.

CHAPTER-THIRTY-THREE
Dad's Family

Mom didn't just keep us away from our dad but also from his parents and family. I've since met many cousins and have learned some really positive inspiring things about my father. Our cousins together with my dad spent many years in search of us and share about the many trips they took in pursuit of me and my sisters. They tell stories that on most weekends our father would pick them up and they would actually drive up and down the streets of Los Angeles in search of "his" girls. They said that as soon as we were found we moved to a new location. My sisters and I didn't know how often dad had located us, but he must have made contact with mom or she wouldn't have known that it was time to move again.

Once after dad found out where we lived, he waited until mother went to work and came over, picked us up and took us out for the day. Unfortunately, mother came home early that day and we all got a beating. I was about four years old. Another time, as I was in the tub I heard a knock on the door and recognized my daddy's voice; I stood on the edge to try to see him, slipped and cracked my head open. The next thing I remember is coming home from the hospital.

Once I was walking down the street with mother, I

saw my daddy walking toward us from the opposite direction, I was so excited and when he reached us he got down on one knee to greet and hug me; he took my little hands and filled them with all the sparkly coins that he had. Mother yanked me away and kept walking. She knew more ways to break my heart; like the time we saw daddy at the movies with another women, mother made it a point to tell me that if he loved me he wouldn't be with someone else. After these events dad was never able to find us again.

My cousins share wonderful insight about our father. They say that he was the best uncle that they could have asked for. He taught Ben how to cook, especially how to make the famous New Mexico Red Chile. My cousin David tells me that his long career with The Boy's Scouts of America was inspired, promoted and encouraged by our dad. They say that he was an excellent role model.

Dad had three brothers and one sister; we're told that they were all great parents, uncles and aunt. Today, I received my first photo of my paternal grandmother. My cousin sent me a long awaited photo of our grandmother and she's wearing a HAT. Those of you who know me personally know that I love hats and I wear them often. If you looked at our home you'd find them in cabinets, closets, on walls, hat racks and even under the bed. You would see an assortment of classic cowboy hats, straw, felt, berets, cloches, pill box, and even fascinators in my jewelry cabinet.

Isn't God the coolest! He has given me a positive role model to connect with. Nothing in God's kingdom is by chance because he is sovereign over everything.

CHAPTER THIRTY-FOUR
Missed Opportunities

Throughout my life the Holy Spirit has walked with me to accomplish what I perceived to be impossible. It's as though my hands and my mind have been guided by an invisible force and at times taken over by angels. I'm amazed as I review my past and know that what I've done could not have been entirely by my own doing.

In design school I received numerous design awards from college and even from a tri-city sponsored contest. Early on I was blessed with the ability to create both in the interior and fashion design worlds.

I passed on an amazing career opportunity to do some design work for some of the wealthiest Quakers in Whittier, CA. The design firm that wanted to hire me painted a glorious picture for anyone that is considering Interior Design as a profession. It was a dream come true but would require me to travel domestically and globally for about one to two weeks each month.

My sons were very young, two and four years old. I would need to get a live-in caregiver, I couldn't do that to them. With my upbringing so screwy I couldn't trust them with anyone other myself. I passed it all up with the hope that I'd get another chance.

Shortly after I married Steve came another career

dream of a lifetime. Everyone in the clothing industry submits resumes in hopes of finding their dream job in New York's famous garment district. I never applied or send out my resume but through a referral I was contacted about an exciting opportunity. That opportunity arrived for me three weeks after we got married.

I had garnered numerous design awards and that is what got me on the who's who list of potential invitees. I couldn't believe it, Steve in New York City would be a joke. He moved out west to be near the Pacific Ocean and ride his jet ski. I didn't even know how to mention it much less consider a move.

If God isn't testing me he must have a better plan. I reminded him that time is passing me by. My spiritual growth was never diminished by whatever was happening in the secular world. I've learned to ask for things differently so maybe I don't have to wait until I'm ninety to reach my castle in the sky to delight in the sweet pleasures that God has waiting for me. I submit to only his purpose and whatever happens after that is fine by me.

CHAPTER THIRTY-FIVE
My Fantasy World

I lived with many fantasies and one of my favorites was escaping from my crib and I'd run away wearing diapers and my little white flannel shirt with the delicate little embroidered flowers around the neckline. I'd find a bus bench and hide underneath it, but have no idea how I knew about bus benches. Jesus would come along, extend his hand for me to reach up and take it, he would smile and we would walk away together. It was a wonderful fantasy and so pleasant.

Another one was my mini horse corral. There were several little horses no bigger than my dog, a Maltese named Chardonnay. The horses were only about twelve inches tall. I'd watch them play for long periods of time. They were so small and cute, they would jump and play but could never hurt me. I've loved horses my whole life and am no longer afraid of the big ones, though they can be a little intimidating as they are so much bigger than my fantasy horses.

When I moved to New Mexico I vowed that I'd learn to horseback ride. I've taken a few lessons and I have a few interesting stories about that.

When I was about six or seven we had a neighbor named Candy. We were the same age but she was a spoiled brat.

She had a wonderful mother and a grandmother that lived with them. I'd watch her through the window mistreating both of them and fantasize about what it'd be like to have a great mom and grandma in my life. I've always envied friends who have had great parents. I know that is wrong and a sin but I desperately wanted a loving, nurturing mother.

Remember when I first met the team from Sophia Fellowship I fantasized about being loved by a whole healthy wonderful man. I would eventually receive numerous proposals by wonderful emotionally healthy men.

CHAPTER-THIRTY-SIX
The Barbershop Café

We have now been in New Mexico for over seventeen years. We moved to New Mexico and started a Café from scratch called The Barbershop Café. We ran this endeavor for fifteen years and met a lot of great people. As I said, Carrie is a wonderful chef and various family members have been in the restaurant or food industry. Our café was very popular and we received accolades and reviews from many different sources, one came from as far away as the Los Angeles Times newspaper. In the August 2004 edition of Sunset Magazine they reviewed The Barbershop Café and made the following summary "One of the finest cafes in New Mexico, period. Our favorite: slow roasted brisket. The desserts such as the New Orleans bread pudding with bourbon sauce, could be offered as prizes in the state lottery". We've catered for Ted Turner and other celebrities who shall remain anonymous and hosted wonderful parties. It's been over two years since we closed and took a sabbatical leave. We still get contacted on a regular basis with inquiries and requests for catering or "when are you going to open the restaurant again"?

Carrie got married in 2004, moved away and we continued to keep the restaurant open another eleven years after she left. Operating a small business, especially a food establishment is daunting and there is never time to do anything else. In the food service industry you need to be open on the days that the general population is available to your establishment so we were open on Sunday. By being open we could never attend church, bible study or anything else on a regular basis. Since closing we have found a wonderful spirit filled church here in a local town called Caballo.

The cook book that I wrote included all of the recipes we used in the café with many modifications in order for them to be the best with the minimum of ingredients. This cook book came primarily due to requests from customers for recipes and inspiration. For my second edition I'm including new recipes and making the usual corrections that many books require. In the first copy I created several recipes that were "gluten free" due to the need at that time. Now there are now an abundant amount of alternate wheat free flours available and they can be substituted equally in a cup for cup measurement in most recipes.

While I cooked and prepared the food I prayed or asked for a blessing for customers. Since we offered specials, I regularly consulted with the Holy Spirit for inspiration. Sometimes when you're creating anything, whether it's food, a painting, a piece of jewelry or anything, you are at a loss for ideas; he always came through with the perfect "special" using ingredients that we had on hand. That was critical since the nearest grocery store is forty minutes away.

CHAPTER THIRTY-SEVEN
Prophetic Visions

Since I was a young girl Our Lord has given me a gift of prophecy and visions on a regular basis. Sometimes the meaning is clear, other times I pray, wait and see what the Holy Spirit says to me.

I woke up one morning with a vision of an evergreen tree. To one side of the tree were two oversized avocados and there was one to the left side of it. I knew immediately that the tree represented the same pine tree that is on the "Appeal to Heaven" flag. This flag was flown by the order of George Washington commander in chief of the Continental Army in October 1775. It is a symbol of solidarity, conviction and our present hope for America. The avocados represent spiritual fruit and I believe that the three represented a divided nation. There is promise in that we are still represented in that flag.

The most profound vision that I ever received was in 1983. My sons were eleven and thirteen years old at the time. We walked out the front door together; our front courtyard was enclosed with a rock wall about waist high. It was a beautiful spring day with a lovely clear blue sky; it was a perfect setting for what I was about to witness. The boys took off running through the open gate. I looked up to admire the sky and thank God for his constant blessings.

What I saw took my breath away. Like a clear motion picture I saw two tall skyscrapers and lessor buildings all around. All of a sudden something hit the two tallest buildings and caused a great explosion. The smoke that ensued was a dirty brownish-gray charcoal kind of smoke.

It took me several seconds to register what I had just witnessed. Oh God! My first thought was that a rocket had come from the East and caused the explosion. I wasn't certain what city I was looking at but knew that it wasn't Chicago or Los Angeles as I knew what both of those metropolitan cities looked like and it wasn't either one. I studied photographs of New York City and right then I knew that the buildings hit were the World Trade Center Twin Towers. I still thought that it had to have been a rocket to cause that kind of explosion like maybe a rocket propelled grenade.

I only spoke of this to a few close friends and my immediate family. I wanted to heed some sort of warning but then I thought "who would believe me"? It's clear to us all exactly what happened.

A week before the horrific event of 9/11 I had surreal visions. I'd go to bed and as soon as I closed my eyes I'd see faces. It was as though they were floating like balloons right in front of me. They were faces of Middle East bearded men, some wore turbans while others wore head scarves. I told Steve that I didn't know what it meant but that I couldn't close my eyes without seeing them.

It would be years before we would all learn what that explosion really meant. Only after the news reported and showed photos of the hijackers did I understand the meaning of the secondary vision and how it was related to the first vision that I'd experienced years earlier.

What I perceived as rocket propelled grenades were actually two planes which deliberately targeted buildings on American soil for a catastrophic event such as we've never seen in North America.

Another day I was sitting upstairs in my favorite prayer chair which looks out through a large arched window to trees and a rolling hillside. I was praying and pleading for the safety and protection of Israel and the Lord showed me a vision of the entire state covered by an enormous purple umbrella. He was showing me that Israel will always be under his protection.

When I was pregnant for the third time we were certain that we were having a girl. I was struggling about whether or not to breast feed her because I had problems nursing my sons. I had pain, inflammation and lacked enough milk to keep them satisfied. One evening after I prayed the Lord gave me a beautiful vision. I saw the Blessed Mother nursing Jesus and knew he was telling me that all would be good if I nursed our daughter. He was absolutely right as I went on to nurse her for about 1 ½ years without a single problem such as I'd previously experienced. Our Lord is always present, he is a good, good Father and requires of us, only that we ask and have gratitude for his numerous blessings, so many that each of us could write an entire book detailing his gifts.

CHAPTER THIRTY-EIGHT
Redeem, Forgive and Repent

Recently we had an intercessory prayer meeting at our place of business. It is the same location where the high stakes poker games were played, where the local watering hole was and where my parents celebrated their wedding reception almost eighty years earlier!

We prayed for the redemption of the poker room where my grandfather had lost my grandmother in a card game. We asked Jesus Christ for forgiveness and we repented for all the sins committed because of his gambling addiction.

We reclaimed the land and blessed it with biblical anointing oil. Today we will take communion with the body and blood of Jesus at the property. We will repent for the sins and curses that plagued our parent's relationship right from the start and we will leave all the sins of our bloodline at the cross.

My goal is to help others with their healing so I'm preparing to become a facilitator for Sozo Ministry. You can learn more about Sozo at *www.bethelsozo.com* or at Bethel Church, Redding, California.

CHAPTER THIRTY-NINE
Bonnie

When I started my manuscript my sisters felt that they didn't want to contribute in any way and did not want me to use their real names. In fact they didn't want me to expose any facts related to our upbringing. Bonnie has since decided to share some of her memories. In Bonnie's own words "Reflections of my childhood"-

I don't remember much from my childhood except for a couple of events that occurred when we lived in Hanover, New Mexico. When I was about six years old, I would wake up screaming and crying from horrible nightmares, I'd wake up terrified. My dad would pick me up and comfort me but I would be fighting and hitting him with my little fists. I remember seeing the face of a devil on the bedroom mirror. They would clean it but it always came back.

Mom and dad fought all the time. She would yell and scream at him and he'd ultimately hit her. Once he even put her outside during a winter storm and it wasn't very long after that fight that they separated. We were outside saying goodbye to dad. Angela took it the hardest and she got very sick.

Dad moved to California and from then on we hardly ever saw him. Mother moved us to El Paso,

Texas. We were living in a run down, tiny vacant building that was formerly a café. There were mice all over and I used to play with them. Now I think how disgusting that was.

While living in El Paso when I was about seven or eight years old, I had a growth on my upper gum. I needed to see a doctor or a dentist so mother put me on a bus to get to the dentist. I got lost taking the wrong bus and exited in the wrong place. It was a terrible experience as I don't remember how or when I got home.

We didn't live in El Paso very long. Our next move was to Las Cruces where mother placed us in an orphanage for a while. I liked being there because they would take us places in a big truck. We all had lice. We had two uniforms, one for Sunday and another for the rest of the week. Our next move was to Los Angeles.

Mom was very controlling, powerful, mentally abusive, and strict and we only spoke when we were asked to speak. We got routinely punished whether we deserved it or not. Life was brutal but it was worse for Angela, like a curse.

If mother had not been controlling and powerful where would we be today? I imagine much worse. Mom kept us out of foster homes or from becoming permanent orphans. She was tough and I don't regret any of it. I have no anger, only love for my mother.

When we were living in Los Angeles we moved frequently. My cousin says that our dad was always looking for us. One time dad came for us when mom was at work. When she got home we all got a beating even Angela and she was only about four years old. We rarely saw him after that.

Growing up without our father was very sad. Mother was always working, or gone, we were young and were left with our oldest sister who was about nine years old. I believe that mother did the best that she was capable of.

My sisters and I were all good and innocent. The way I see it now, my sisters and I turned out to be exceptional women, good mothers and very independent. I am seventy-five years old and it has taken me this long to start growing. I know God loves us and was always protecting us.

Bonnie

CHAPTER FORTY
My Best Friend Jesus

I knew at an early age that I have a Father in Heaven that loves me very much. I knew through faith that Jesus was with me no matter what was going on in my life. I often questioned his motive for bringing me to such a cruel and unloving place.

I feared everything, puppies, horses, and even tadpoles terrified me. I've spend a lot of time repenting since I learned that fear is a sin and very toxic to one's wellbeing.

Most people have some kind of fear. Fear of illness, insecurity, finances, aging, abandonment and disease reflects our health. By repenting and asking Christ for forgiveness our overall health will improve. We need to remind ourselves constantly that when Jesus was crucified he took all, not some, but all our pain and suffering with him so that we might live to the fullest with blessings that we can't even begin to comprehend. Let's remember his promise "on earth as it is in Heaven".

Though there were constant ups and down's I remained committed to my life with Christ. He never left my side as he was the one constant positive thing that I had going on.

We attended Catholic mass on Sundays but it was on my own that I searched out as I reached for more of

Jesus. I made my first communion and confirmation but the yearning for more continued and I couldn't quench my thirst.

I keep a crucifix in our home as a reminder that he died for my sins, our sins. A reminder that no matter how much turbulence there is in my life there is no comparison with what Our Lord encountered nailed to that cross.

My safe place was Jesus; he was, is and always will be my saving grace. Throughout my life especially when I was deep in my healing journey I've been inspired to write poetry or sometimes simply one-liners. I hope that this selection blesses you as I have been blessed. I received these one-liners and many more in 1983 and I am usually awakened around 3 am. These primarily came to me while I was at my emotional worst. You could say I was a basket case.

"Lord, you gave me moonbeams to hang on and dreams to capture".

"You helped me to believe in myself".

"Freedom is the beginning of a new soul"

"I listened to the music of your heart and was touched by the sensitivity of your soul".

"Thank you for allowing me into your world even before you existed".

"I will call you and nudge gently. If you send me away I understand"

"My work is not the easiest but you'll know when there is no other way".

"In a man's sensitivity you feel his gentleness; in his

tears you sense his strength".

"I Am Lord of your life, thank you".

"I am a gentle and loving spirit, I will not harm you".

"Hold fast to dreams, for if dreams die, life is a broken winged bird that cannot fly".

"Invite me in I come as a guest".

"My Angels, you have entertained".

"Listen, even the wind speaks".

"Soar to the farthest reaches of my world".

From John the harbinger I received these words "in beauty will you spread the word".

"It is I that dwells within who creates your beauty".

"You will come to know the many rooms in my mansion"

"I'm having a love affair with the Lord, through osmosis he'll reach the others".

"At times I can see forever, the vastness of my world proclaims the greatness of my Master, my Father, my Creator.

A seascape, a landscape

How does one encompass the universe?

A chill, a tear, my body's a tingle

The warm sun absorbs me into itself,

thank you Father, and thank you for me".

"I am but one fish in the pond yet the entire school responds".

My favorite inspired one liner "You will build your own ark"

I didn't comprehend this one until 2005 (the same year that mother got ill) when a pastor visited our home that Steve built. The first thing he said was "this is an ark"!

How is that for awesomeness?

Epilogue

This story is about the resiliency of women. I wouldn't change anything that has happened to me. I've come out strong and powerful in ways that I never expected. I've learned that women are the heart, soul and strength of the family; we fall but rise up again, stronger and more determined with a solid faith in a loving Father and Creator that is the cornerstone of everything in our lives.

Though my journey has been toilsome, I've been blessed to experience things that I otherwise would have circumvented; I wouldn't be where I am today had I taken any shortcuts. Through each painful step I refused to be in denial about the challenges that presented themselves; if not me to change family dynamics, then who? I've met wonderfully pious, and humble mentors along the way; women who have taught me to live my life with truth, dignity and integrity. My constant companion has never led me astray even when I was angry at our Lord or non-deserving of his grace and mercy.

My mind and heart are open to help others that may be in bondage. I'm particularly interested in helping those who are violated through the sex trafficking industry or the innocence of children taken away by pedophiles, and or family members.

Today I spend days in the company of my husband

and good, good friends that I admire and respect. I was reluctant to write my story fearing that I would somehow be judged but the opposite has happened; my husband and friends have rallied around me to say we love you more than ever.

While writing my story I've been able to see some personal growth taking place in Bonnie's life. She's taking baby steps; it's a tough journey but I'm very proud of her.

I can be contacted at Treasuredsilence@yahoo.com or by mail at PO Box 485, Hillsboro, NM 88042.

Angela

www.ingramcontent.com/pod-product-compliance
Lightning Source LLC
Chambersburg PA
CBHW032043290426
44110CB00012B/927